PEI Guide to
Word processing

Second edition

Anne Allan

Pitman Publishing

PITMAN PUBLISHING
128 Long Acre, London, WC2E 9AN

A Division of Longman Group UK Limited

© Annetta Perry 1990
© Longman Group UK Limited 1993

First published in Great Britain 1990
Second edition 1993

British Library Cataloguing in Publication Data

A CIP catalogue record for this book is available on request from the
British Library

ISBN 0 273 60002 8

Typeset in 10/13pt Futura Light by Edna A. Moore, ⚡ Tek-Art,
Addiscombe, Croydon, Surrey
Printed and bound in Great Britain

Contents

How to use this guide

This guide is designed to provide **practice** and **support** for candidates preparing for entry to the Pitman Elementary, Intermediate, Advanced and Masterclass Word Processing examinations. These examinations are not limited to particular software packages and, similarly, this guide is not limited to specific software but can be used to learn and practise the various functions of many different packages.

An effective operator of word processing systems never stops learning new information and practising its application to develop new skills. For personal satisfaction and for the benefit of employers, the acquisition of new skills can be proven by passing examinations. When facing examinations, candidates have a number of resources — apart from their own abilities — which they can call upon for help. Instruction and access to different word processing systems in an instructional setting are obviously very important.

Those teachers and trainers who are responsible for such courses will, in turn, have their own sources such as the Pitman Examinations Institute's *Word Processing — Examinations Guide* and *Marking Guide — Elementary Word Processing** and their contribution will represent an important input.

However, aspiring candidates should be interested to gain direct access to the knowledge which they will be required to show, to give examples of its application and take up opportunities to demonstrate their own acquisition and application of this knowledge against the criteria of assessment which they will face during examinations.

Part 1 of this guide assumes that candidates will have already acquired the following *basic skills*, to which they will be seeking to add through practice and knowledge in preparation for the Pitman Examinations Institute Elementary Examination in Word Processing:

- switch on and load the operating and word processing applications program
- access the file directory
- create a *new* file
- store a file to disk
- recall a previously stored file from disk
- print a file from disk
- operate the keyboard, including figures, shift and fractions
- appreciate the operation of the function or control key which, when pressed, makes the computer carry out word processing instructions
- operate the cursor control/arrow keys
- exit from the word processing applications program
- exit from the operating program
- switch off the system

Part 2 is designed for those candidates who have already acquired the level of skill dealt with in Part 1, which they should have demonstrated either by satisfactory completion of some of the Part 1 final examination assessments, or by going through the checklist provided on pages 4–5 to ensure that all elements of the Elementary Syllabus have been covered. Likewise, Parts 3 and 4 should only be attempted by candidates who are competent in the previous sections.

The design of the guide should enable individual candidates to experience the way in which the components of a skill can be *identified, practised and assessed* and then brought together in stages to form a new level of competence.

This step-by-step approach has the clear goal of preparing candidates both to be competent word processor operators in the work situation and to pass their chosen word processing examination successfully.

*Available from PEI, Catteshall Manor, GODALMING, Surrey GU7 1UU

Each step contains:

- **objectives** which provide a clear outline of the skills or competences to be achieved
- an **example** which clarifies these objectives
- **test your competence** which provides an opportunity to check on the ability to carry out this objective
- **practice from the paper** which provides further realistic practice of the objective taken from a past Pitman Examinations Institute examination paper

All Parts of the guide contain a **complete past paper** at the appropriate level. These past questions will enable students to appreciate that success in any examination is aided by an awareness of what is commonly called 'examination technique'. The guide therefore concludes with recommendations in word processing examination technique. Further past papers and specimen papers may be obtained from Pitman Examinations Institute.

Finally, a **checklist for candidates**, which may be photocopied, is provided at all levels. It is suggested that candidates use these checklists to record their progress and to ensure full coverage of the stated requirements of the examination. If a function or task has been carried out successfully, either with assistance or unaided, then this should be recorded in the appropriate column and the date added.

For those candidates who are unfamiliar with or wish to confirm examples of acceptable layout for those business documents generally used in the Pitman Examinations Institute Word Processing examinations, a **reference section** is included in the *Appendix*. This provides a useful reference point and aid to fulfilling the essential requirement of presenting tasks, which relate to a variety of business documents, in *correct* and *acceptable* form.

Part 1 **Elementary**

Instructions for Part 1

The various stages leading to *competence* in word processing operations are broken down so that the skill is first *identified*, then *practised* using example material and an extract from a past PEI examination paper in word processing, and finally competence is checked using self or peer assessment. The areas of knowledge and skills acquisition covered follow the sequence set out in the **checklist** on pages 4 and 5. However, if you are already competent in some of the areas, then you may select a particular area on a 'pick and mix' basis according to your personal requirements.

It is suggested that you maintain a **portfolio** of your work with a copy of the checklist for recording your progress.

Syllabus

(Time allowed – 1 hour – excluding printing time, plus 5 minutes for reading.)

The skill of word processing, like that of typewriting, is essentially practical. This examination is aimed at candidates seeking a first qualification in Word Processing, testing their ability to use a word processing machine to perform a given range of tasks. The candidate will be tested in a combination of speed, accuracy and presentation of material which is common to the majority of business offices using a word processing facility.

The examination will consist of 4 tasks on a common theme, using documents which have been prepared and filed on the storage medium by the Specialist Teacher.

Candidates must attempt every question and at least some part of each question must be submitted, otherwise the candidate will automatically fail. The candidate should be able to:

1   Create a new document and save it on the storage medium.

2   Type and display effectively a variety of business documents from handwritten or typewritten drafts. These might include:

   a business letter
   a document requiring tabulation
   a menu
   a notice
   an advertisement
   an article or report.

3   Plan the layout of material.

4   Respond to written instructions and printers' correction signs.

5   Plan and organise work within the time constraint.

6   Retrieve and edit a document.

7   Insert, delete and move text.

8   Use underscore, centring and tabulation facilities.

9   Revise a document containing 'deliberate mistakes'.

10   Retrieve a standard document and complete manually with items of variable information.

11   Proof-read and correct on screen as necessary.

12   Proof-read typed work against the original for accuracy and layout.

13   Print documents on either single sheet or continuous stationery in an acceptable format.

Assessment

The examination will consist of 4 tasks on a common theme containing approximately 300 words of input in total to be completed in 1 hour 5 minutes.

Candidates' performance will be assessed on the criteria of accuracy, presentation and production rate.

Candidates must attempt all four required tasks and to be awarded a **Pass** grade must achieve a 95% standard of accuracy and no more than 8 presentation errors.

A **First Class Pass** will be awarded if candidates achieve a 98% standard of accuracy and no more than 4 presentation errors.

Conducting the examination

The Specialist Teacher must prepare the candidates' examination material in advance of the examination. For this reason, the Examinations Secretary, in the presence of the Specialist Teacher, may open the envelope containing the examination material in advance of the day of the examination. Under no circumstances must the Specialist Teacher be given a copy of the examination paper. On completion of the preparation, the examination material must be resealed and lodged with the Examinations Secretary for safe-keeping. The *Instructions to Candidates* sheets must be completed **only** by the Specialist Teacher. On no account may they be completed by the candidates themselves. These sheets form part of the examination paper and must be returned to the Institute after the examination.

Where an examination paper requires the candidate to recall a copy of the text creation task to use as the text revision task, the Centre may allow the candidate to print the text creation task and then use that work as the basis for the text revision task. The timing of the examination for that candidate may be suspended during this printing and the separate parts of the examination timing should be shown on the *Attestation Form*.

Checklist – Elementary

		Aided	Date	Unaided	Date
1	**First steps in word processing**				
	Log on/start up the equipment				
	Create new document file				
	Save both a new and an edited file to disk				
	Print out documents				
	Log off/close down the system				
2	**Setting margins** Create text by setting margins of minimum 1"/2.5 cm or as instructed.				
3	**Using the tab key** Create text by using the tab key to display text in columns.				
4	**Printers' correction signs** Create text from the author's original which contains amendments and respond to the printers' correction signs used.				
5	**Underlining** Change the display of a document by using the underline facility for headings and words within the text.				
6	**Centring text** Change the display of a document by using the centre facility to centre lines of text.				
7	**Spaced and closed capitals** Change the display of a document by using spaced and closed capitals.				
8	**Line spacing and format** Ensure consistency of line spacing. Justified and ragged right margin.				
9	**Inserting text** Edit or revise a document file by using the insert facility to insert characters, words, phrases, sentences, lines and paragraphs within existing text. Retrieve previously stored documents.				
10	**Deleting text** Edit or revise a document file by using the delete facility to delete characters, words, phrases, sentences, lines and paragraphs within existing text (either with or without replacing text).				
11	**Joining and splitting paragraphs** Edit or revise a document file by joining or splitting paragraphs.				
12	**Moving text** Edit or revise a document file by using the move facility to move text within a single document.				

13	**Presenting documents in an acceptable style** Present in correct and acceptable form standard business documents, responding to printers' correction signs and using a currently acceptable style of presentation.				
14	**Inserting variable information** Recall a standard document from disk and create a final document by keying in variable information at in-fill points.				
15	**Proof-reading onscreen and against copy** Proof-read onscreen a document containing obvious keying in errors of agreement, punctuation and line spacing and recognise and correct errors. Proof-read against copy a document that you have recalled or edited and recognise and correct errors.				
16	**Elementary examination questions** Ensure that all competences learned so far meet the required standard for the Elementary examination.				

1 First steps in word processing

The following is a list of basic procedures to be achieved in word processing
- *log-on/start-up* equipment
- *create* a document file
- use the *default* or pre-set margins
- *key in* text using text wraparound, ie *not* using the carriage return at line-endings
- use RETURN key twice between paragraphs in order to leave a clear line space between these
- *store* a document file to disk
- *print* a document file
- *log-off/close down equipment*

Example

```
CARE OF DISKS

Disks should be well maintained.  The
exposed area of the disk should not be
touched at any time.  Fingerprints
could obstruct the disk drive from
reading the disk.  NEVER bend the disk.

For reference, label all your disks
with self-adhesive labels.  Write on
the label before adhering.  If
necessary write on the disk with felt
tip pen as penetration from a pen or
pencil could damage the disk.

Do not leave the disk in direct
sunlight.
```

Text wrapped by system

Clear line space between paragraphs

Test your competence

Start up your equipment and create a new document file. Using *default* (pre-set) margins, key in the text from the above example and store the file on disk. Print one copy of the file and then close down your equipment.

Practice from the paper

Open a new document file and key in the following using the *default* margins. Store and print one copy.

```
PASSPORTS AND VISAS

For a holiday abroad you will need a valid passport, and
you should check carefully that it is valid for the entire
duration of your holiday and for the country you are
visiting.

If you have to apply for a new passport, this should be
done at least four weeks before your departure date.  The
Passport Office inform us that during April and August
applications take longer than at other times of the year,
so do think ahead.

For certain countries of the world, a visa or visitor's
pass is required.  Should this apply to the country which
you are visiting, details will be sent to you with your
final invoice.
```

Check your success

Can you log on/start up the equipment? ☐

Can you create a document file? ☐

Did you allow the text to wrap at the right margin? ☐

Did you use the Return key *twice* between paragraphs? ☐

Did you store the file to disk? ☐

Did you print the file successfully? ☐

Did you proof-read your document? ☐

2   Setting margins

Create text by setting margins of minimum 1"/2.5 cm or as instructed

When creating a new file at the Elementary level you will not be required to set different margins from the default margins, unless these produce margins of less than 1"/2.5 cm.

Most systems have a **status line** which is located either at the top or the bottom of the screen. This line gives the operator useful information about the page layout that you have chosen. On some systems a **ruler line** is also displayed which shows the location of the left and right margin and the position of tab stops.

Example

The following text has been keyed in using margins of 10 and 70 giving a typing line of 60 characters. A **blocked style** has been used for the paragraphs.

The printout is in 10 pitch, ie 10 characters to the inch.

_L_   _R_

_10_   _70_

```
As I have set the margins for the exercise at 10 and 70 and
I am using 10 pitch, when I print out the file, as long as
the print-head is set to start printing at the far left edge
of the paper, my work will print out with a left margin of
1"/2.5 cm and the same at the right.

I have used the carriage return twice between the blocked
style of paragraphs to leave a clear line space.
```

Test your competence

Start up your equipment and create a new document file. Use left and right margins of 1"/2.5 cm. Key in the following text using _blocked paragraphs_. Proof-read carefully and print out one copy.

Note: There are 12 character spaces to the inch in 12 pitch and 10 character spaces to the inch in 10 pitch. Some type fonts are proportionally spaced. This means that all letters have the same amount of white space around them and so letters take up different amounts of space, eg letter **m** takes up more space than letter **i**. The number of characters along a line varies depending on the letters and the font used. Compare this text (which is proportionally spaced) with the exercise that you are about to type (which is not proportionally spaced). Size of characters can be measured in point size – the larger the number, the larger the size of the character in that font.

Make sure that you know which pitch or point size you are in.

As you begin to operate your word processor you will find the command structure very simple to use. The structure is conversational, meaning that each time you give a command the operator prompt line will assist you through the various stages.

The sort of information that is displayed on the status line includes the disk number, the name of the document, the mode of operation of the machine, the cursor indicator, line indicator, line spacing and pitch.

The ruler or format line indicates the margins, tabs or other specification for the particular document.

Practice from the paper

Open a new document file and key in the following using margins of 1"/2.5 cm. Save and print one copy.

Well Green Golf Club has enjoyed a culture of courtesy and friendship since its inception, and expects a high standard of behaviour both on and off the course.

Proposers of new members have a responsibility under the Constitution of the Club to ensure that they are properly introduced to the game and to the Club. On joining the Club, all new members are expected to familiarise themselves with the etiquette of play, as specified in the Rules of Golf, and to observe these on the course.

Club staff are expected to behave courteously to members at all times, as are members to them. On no account may a member instruct or reprimand a member of staff directly.

Check your success

Did you open a new document file? ☐

Did you use margins of 1"? ☐

Did you follow the copy exactly, leaving a clear line space between paragraphs? ☐

Did you follow the use of *capital* letters exactly? ☐

Did you proof-read carefully? ☐

3 Using the tab key

How to use the tab key to set out information displayed in columns

As previously mentioned, typical word processing equipment displays a **status line** which gives information about the spacing, pitch, file name, page number etc. The **ruler line**, if visible, shows the position of the left and right margins and the tab settings. The tabs are often pre-set at intervals of 5 character spaces. The ruler line is visible on the screen but does not print out with your hard copy.

If you wish to set tab stops at positions which differ from the pre-set or *default* tab settings then it is a good idea to *clear* the existing tabs to give a clear ruler line. New tabs can then be set and can be clearly seen without causing confusion.

Information set out in columns at the Elementary level involves keying in either 2 or 3 columns of text or figures. The tab key is used to set a *fixed point* which is reached by pressing the **tab** key and provides quick access to the starting point of each column.

When setting out information in this way you must remember to allow for the *longest* item in each column (whether this is the column heading or within the body of the text) followed by an *equal* amount of space *between* the columns.

The tabulated material in the Elementary examination is usually contained within a document. When this is the case the first column usually starts flush with the left margin, ie using the **blocked style**, and is *not* centred.

A simple procedure would be to:

1   type first item of first column at left margin
2   press the space bar once for each letter, allowing sufficient space for the longest item in that column and for the spaces to be left between (eg 3 or 5 spaces)
3   set a tab at this point
4   repeat steps 2 and 3 for each column

Example

The following material has been keyed in using 10 pitch and margins of 10 and 70. Tabs have been set at 40 and 52.

```
L                                       T           T                   R
10                                      40          52                  70
```

```
The following information should assist you in deciding on
the materials you require for the patio and garden extension you
are proposing:

                              SIZE        PRICE

Heavy Square Mesh Trellis     6' x 1'     £4.99
Square Wall Trellis           6' x 1'     £4.60
Fan Trellis                   6' x 1'     £3.65
```

Note space before and after 'x'

Start up your equipment and create a new document file. Use left and right margins of 1"/2.5 cm and set tabs at the appropriate position to line up the columns of text.

Please find a list of the students concerned and their particular area of interest:

NAME	COURSE
Raymond Lo	HND Electronics
Fiona Hung	Business Studies
Linda Lui	BTEC National Computing
Ho Wing-Lei	Personal Assistant
Li Ming Tai	EFL
Phoebe Lam	Secretarial

Practice from the paper

Open a new document file and key in the following.

Would you please note that the following dates have been reserved for the social events planned at the last meeting:

Leave 1 clear line space only

Saturday 3 November	7.00	pm	Bonfire Party
Wednesday 24 November	8.00	pm	Bridge Drive
Saturday 1 December	8.30	pm	Supper Drive
Saturday 22 December	3.00	pm	Children's Party
Monday 31 December	8.30	pm	New Year's Eve

Check your success

Did you copy the layout exactly? ☐

Did you leave *one clear line space* only? ☐

Did you leave equal space between the columns? ☐

Did you leave space before 'pm'? ☐

Are your dates and times accurate? ☐

Practice from the paper

Open a new document file and key in the following. *Copy the layout exactly*. Save to disk and print one copy.

Orders are being taken for the following:

Single line spacing

T-shirts	Short-sleeved, white with motif in red	£2.75
Sweaters	Long-sleeved, acrylic, grey with black	£12.00
Ties	Navy blue with Orchestra motif in red	£3.50

Obtainable by post from the Membership Office, or from foyer displays at concerts.

Check your success

Did you set out the information in 3 columns with equal space between each? ☐

Did you follow the instruction to use single-line spacing? ☐

Did you put a capital 'O' for Orchestra? ☐

Did you use a capital 'M' and 'O' for Membership Office? ☐

Did you leave a clear line space before and after the table? ☐

Did you proof-read carefully? ☐

Did you *align* the decimal points in the money? ☐

4 Printers' correction signs

Creating a file from author's original which contains amendments using printers' correction signs

A new document file is often created from the author's *handwritten* original. The author often makes amendments to this handwritten version using **printers' correction signs**. The following are examples:

Sign within text	Marginal instruction	Meaning
[	N P	start new paragraph
⌐	run on	join two paragraphs
ʎ	ʎ	insert text here
∿	trs	change the order of the words and figures
〔 〕	trs	change the position vertically
~~Monday~~	stet	retain the word crossed out with the dotted line beneath
~~Wednesday~~	ð	delete text
pitman	u c	use upper case
Child or ¢hild	lc	use lower case
[ ]➚		move block of text

Examples   The typed text which follows has been keyed in following the author's amendments.

Amended text

---

uc   Once again it is aGM time, which
stet   ~~usually~~ heralds changes, and these
my∧   will be revealed as/report unfolds.   run on
          This last year has been a |one| trs
trs   (dynamic) encompassing several
          milestones which characterise the
          rigour of Branch Activities. [The
s∧   informal dinner meeting/ seminars
          and visits have resulted in a new
          record of attendance by members and·
∂]   ~~gyests~~ guests.

          Attendance 1988-89 was over 1,000/   ⊙∧
trs   Attendance 1987-88 was over 850.

Keyed in version

Once again it is AGM time, which
usually heralds changes, and these
will be revealed as my report
unfolds. This last year has been a
dynamic one encompassing several
milestones which characterise the
rigour of Branch Activities.

The informal dinner meetings,
seminars and visits have resulted in
a new record of attendance by
members and guests.

Attendance 1987-88 was 850.
Attendance 1988-89 was over 1,000.

Test your competence   Open a new document file using left and right margins of 1"/2.5 cm. Key in the following text, observing the printers' correction signs. Proof-read the text carefully and store on disk. Print out one copy.

uc   Your Branch is now a member of the <u>w</u>arminster Chamber of
run on   Commerce. ⌐
and services
of   ⌐Members can enjoy these <u>facilities</u>/through those nominated
stet   committee members by ~~contacting~~ approaching the Branch Secretary.
NP   The committee is represented on the WCAN committee which
lc   is currently involved in an <u>I</u>nitiative headed 'A COMMON
        PURPOSE FOR OUR TOWNS'.

trs   1989 is the 25th anniversary of the Branch.
        1988 was a record pre-anniversary year for the Branch.

Practice from the paper

Open a new document file and key in the following *using the layout indicated*. File your completed document and print one copy.

IONITHERMIE

and ^ This is a revolutionary new/treatment for Cellulite, which has
effective been widely and favourably publicised in the national press.

Most women suffer from having fat deposits on certain parts
of the body, and any amount of dieting will not ~~bring about~~ involve   stet
the required reduction of those particular areas. Re-shaping
of the figure is required - not general weight-loss. ⌐

run on   ⌐This new Cellulite treatment gives a greater degree of control
trs   over ⌐shaping⌐figure⌐ than dieting can, and the manufacturers
lc   claim that the treatment also <u>R</u>ejuvenates the skin.

of   Many women suffer embarrassment from unsightly fat deposits,
     at some time in their lives - particularly after child-birth
     or in 'middle age'. This can cause anxiety and lead to a
     state of severe depression.

Check your success

Did you follow the instructions given? ☐

Did you carry out all the amendments successfully? ☐

Did you carefully proof-read your final version on screen? ☐

Does your printout have margins of 1"/2.5 cm at left and right? ☐

5 Underscore (underlining)

Change the display of a document by using the underscore facility to underscore headings and words within the body of the text

The **underscore** facility is used to add emphasis to either a heading or text within the body of a document. When using the underscore facility it is important to underline both the *words* and the *spaces between the words*.

You will need to position the cursor at the beginning of the text to be underlined and key in the appropriate command to underline the amount of text, eg word, line, sentence or paragraph.

While some systems display the underscored text *on the screen*, others use **embedded commands**, ie a command sequence is used to switch on the underscore at the point of the cursor and then a further command is used to switch it off at the appropriate location. With this method the underscore is not visible on the screen so it is *essential* to carry out the second step in the command procedure, otherwise the underscore will underscore *all* the text which follows the first instruction.

If the embedded command facility only underscores words and not the spaces between, then the __ key (underscore) on the keyboard should be used to give an underscore between the words.

Example

KOWLOON CHAMBER OF COMMERCE

The Chamber has meeting facilities and committees to which we may be asked from time to time to provide co-opted members to cover such matters as taxation, education, publicity and PR.

Test your competence

Open a new document file and, using default margins, key in the following text. Use the underscore facility to emphasise the heading and text within the body of the document as indicated. Proof-read carefully and store on disk. Print out one copy.
Note: It is generally accepted that final punctuation (eg full stop at the end of a sentence) is not underlined.

OPEN LUNCHES

The committees take it in turns to host Open Lunches which are held at the New World Hotel on the third Wednesday of each month, 12.30 to 2.00 pm.

ALL MEMBERS ARE WELCOME.

Practice from the paper

Open a new document file and key in the following text. Use the underscore facility to emphasise the heading and part of the text. Store and print out one copy.

<u>PLANTWELL GUIDE</u> – February Issue

For a really colourful, hardy hedging, we have been experimenting with <u>Fuschia Riccartonii</u>, and have been most impressed by its fast growth and flowering splendour.

<u>Dollar Princess</u>, <u>Lena</u> and <u>Beacon</u> are all varieties which are ideal as summer bedding plants.

Check your success

Did you underscore both the words and spaces? ☐

Did you turn off the underscore facility before the punctuation, eg the comma in the first paragraph? ☐

Did you follow the 'copy' *exactly*? ☐

Did you leave a space either side of the *dash* in the heading? ☐

6 Centring text

Change the display of a document by using the centring facility to centre lines of text

The centring facility is one of the automatic functions which can help you to present your work in a pleasing manner very rapidly.

Some systems require you to centre each line individually whereas others allow you to request the system to centre a line, several lines, a paragraph or the entire text.

Headings or text will be centred over the length of the typing line chosen, rather than the width of the page. If you wish the headings to be centred on the page then *equal margins* must be set.

Example

```
           BENEFITS OF MEMBERSHIP

              Export Services
            Information Services
          Local Employer Networks
              Advice Services
         Telex and Bureau Facilities
                Seminars
                Clinics
```

Test your competence

Open a new document file and, using default (pre-set) margins, key in the following text. Use the centring facility to centre the complete page. Proof-read carefully and store on disk. Print out one copy.

MENU

Tomato Soup
or
Melon

Roast Chicken
Roast Lamb
Turkey

Roast Potatoes
Green Beans

Chocolate Mousse
or
Apple Pie with Cream

Test your competence

Open a new document file and, using default margins, key in the following text. Use the centring facility to centre the headings as indicated. Proof-read carefully and store on disk. Print out one copy.

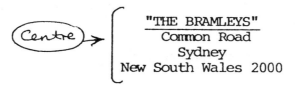

```
                    "THE BRAMLEYS"
                    Common Road
                      Sydney
              New South Wales 2000
```

A superb development of 12 luxury homes to be constructed with a choice of 6 carefully planned designs providing 4 and 5 bedroom accommodation. All completed to a luxurious specification. Each property is set in its own landscaped grounds.

The following plots have been released:

```
Plot 9   The Melbourne
Plot 2   The Canberra
Plot 5   The Claremont
Plot 7   The Queensland
```

Our representative Mr Paul Hutchinson will be resident at our Show House which will be open 7 days a week between 10 am and 5 pm. You will be made very welcome and we know that you will be extremely impressed with the exceptionally high quality of the development.

 SALES OFFICE TELEPHONE NUMBER - SYDNEY 884030

Practice from the paper

Open a new document file and, using left and right margins of 1"/2.5 cm, key in the following text, using the centring facility as required. Proof-read carefully and store on disk. Print out one copy.

THE GOLDEN GIRL HEALTH CENTRE

Sunset Boulevard
Milton Keynes

Whatever your requirements, do call in or telephone for advice -

MILTON KEYNES 650299 ← (centre)

We are pleased to be able to offer the following beauty treatments:

(↓PEDICURE)

(Centre each line)

HAIR - full range of treatments
MANICURE
SUN TANNING
ELECTROLYSIS
BODY MASSAGE
FACIALS
MAKE-UP including eyelash tint/eyebrow re-shape
WAXING

Check your success

Did you centre the main heading? ☐

Did you leave a clear line space between the first line of the heading and the second? ☐

Did you centre the telephone number? ☐

Did you centre the last lines? ☐

Did you insert the word 'pedicure' and centre it? ☐

Did you follow the line spacing given in the copy? ☐

Did you make any keying in errors? ☐

Did you print out the text so that it was positioned attractively on the page? ☐

7 Spaced and closed capitals

Change the display of a document by using spaced and closed capitals

In the PEI Word Processing Examination you will be expected, when creating new text, to follow the original copy or the instructions given as to how to emphasise the headings or information within the body of the text.

Closed capitals are keyed in using the **Caps lock** or **Shift lock** key. On some systems it is possible to give a **command** to request text to be keyed in in capital letters.

Spaced capitals are created by pressing the **spacebar** once after each letter and *3 times between words*. This gives a pleasing effect.

The **underscore** can also be used in combination with headings. Remember to leave a clear line space between headings.

Example

I am writing to remind you that we have been allocated a stand at the forthcoming Trade Fair and I suggest that we meet early next week to discuss arrangements.

Open a new document file and, using default margins, key in the following text. Follow the instructions given and proof-read carefully. Store on disk and print out one copy.

BRITISH EXPO ← Spaced caps

All-British China Show ← CLOSED CAPS and UNDERSCORE

A major exhibition, BRITISH EXPO, is to be staged in BEIJING during NOVEMBER. This important event has been organised jointly by the SINO-BRITISH TRADE COUNCIL and the DTI and has the full support of the China Council for the Promotion of International Trade.

This exhibition will focus Chinese attention firmly on UK products in 3 main areas:

COMMUNICATIONS
FOOD/BEVERAGES
FINANCIAL SERVICES INDUSTRIES

Practice from the paper

Open a new document file and, using margins of 1"/2.5 cm, key in the following. Proof-read carefully and store on disk. Print out one copy.

CRAFTWELL COLLEGE

Course Information   Weekend No 23

COURSE TITLE: PRINCIPLES OF DRAWING

COURSE TUTOR: MARY ANDERSON

This course is intended for people who are convinced that they cannot draw. Many of our regular students on craft courses wish that they had the confidence to create their own designs - for embroidery, wood engraving, glass engraving, etc. This weekend course presents an opportunity to concentrate on the development of an individual style and method of drawing, and the group will be encouraged to consider the function of line and tone through work in a variety of media.

Check your success

Did you use *closed caps* for the first heading? ☐

Did you use *initial capitals* and *underscore* for the next heading? ☐

Did you type 'Weekend No 23' blocked to the right margin? ☐

Did you use *closed capitals* and follow the spacing for the 'Course Title' and 'Course Tutor' headings? ☐

Did you follow *exactly* the spacing given in the copy? □

Did you leave space either side of the *dash*? □

Did you proof-read carefully? □

8   Line spacing and format

Ensure consistency of line spacing and format

It is important that you leave the correct number of line spaces between text. You should get used to judging by eye the number required. To leave 1 clear line space as you are typing, press Return (Enter) twice; to leave 2 clear line spaces, press Return (Enter) 3 times.

At Elementary level you will not be required to alter the printout from the **default ragged right** option whereby the right hand margin remains uneven. This is the type of margin that you have been producing to date. However, you may use a **justified right margin** if you prefer it or if your system defaults to this. Whichever you choose, you must use it throughout the task, ie be consistent.

Example

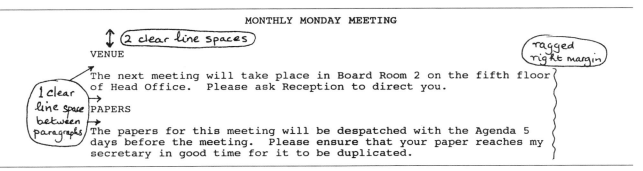

Test your competence

Open a new document file and key in the text, following the line spacing shown. Centre and underscore the heading and then follow other instructions carefully. Save to disk and print out one copy.

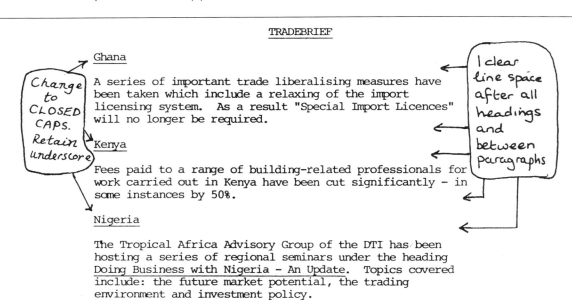

Practice from the paper

Open a new document file and key in the following. Follow the copy exactly and then proof-read carefully onscreen. Save to disk and print out one copy.

leave 2 clear lines of space

LIGHTING AT WORK
NEW HEALTH AND SAFETY EXECUTIVE GUIDANCE } ← (centre and u/s)

It may be hardly noticeable, but lighting can be a serious workplace hazard. There are dozens of different types of light that have to be adapted to thousands of different types of workplace. Yet it is cost or the whim of a designer and not your safety that usually determines the sort of lighting you have.

SAFETY

Bad lighting can increase the number of accidents at work.

Check your success

Did you *centre* each line of the heading? ☐

Did you *underscore* both lines of the heading? ☐

Did you leave the correct number of *line spaces* between sections? ☐

Did you type the headings in *capitals*? ☐

Did you follow the *capitalisation* used? ☐

Did you proof-read carefully? ☐

9 Inserting text

Editing or revising a document file by using the insert facility to insert characters, words, phrases, sentences, lines and paragraphs within existing text

The **insert** facility is used to add characters, words, phrases, sentences, lines of space or paragraphs within an existing document. The need to use the facility can occur either on proof-reading the first version of a document when an omission is noticed, or at the request of the author who indicates amendments to a draft document already stored on disk.

When inserting text you usually need to tell the system:

- that you wish to insert text
- where to start inserting the text, by positioning the cursor at the *point of insertion*
- when to stop inserting

Examples

Single character

r/   The inset facility   The insert facility

String of words

or revising
Editing/text is easy using a word processor

Editing or revising text is easy using a word processor

Sentence

Some word processors have dedicated function keys. ✔You
only have to take your cursor to the appropriate place and
press the key. *The keys are marked with a command, eg INSERT or DELETE.*

Some word processors have dedicated function keys. The
keys are marked with a command, eg INSERT or DELETE. You
only have to take your cursor to the appropriate place and
press the key.

Line space

(leave a clear line space) → EDITING TEXT
Inserting Text

EDITING TEXT

Inserting Text

Paragraph

Some word processors have dedicated function keys. The keys are marked with a command, eg INSERT or DELETE. You only have to take your cursor to the appropriate place and press the key.

(Insert (A) here) →

Sometimes when text is inserted the text extends beyond the right hand margin. In this instance a command has to be given to REFORMAT or tidy up the text.

(A) *If extra blank space is needed then the INSERT facility is used to insert blank lines using the RETURN key. The cursor is positioned at the point at which the space is required.*

Some word processors have dedicated function keys. The keys are marked with a command, eg INSERT or DELETE. You only have to take your cursor to the appropriate place and press the key.

If extra blank space is needed then the INSERT facility is used to insert blank lines using the RETURN key. The cursor is positioned at the point at which the space is required.

Sometimes when text is inserted the text extends beyond the right hand margin. In this instance a command has to be given to REFORMAT or tidy up the text.

Test your competence

Open a new document file and key in the following text, using margins of 1"/2.5 cm. Store on disk. Please copy exactly, including the deliberate error, which has been circled.

INSURANCE DOCUMENTS AND TERMINOLOGY

PROPOSAL

A request to insurers to provide cover.

leave 2 clear line spaces between all sections

POLICY

A document (seting) out the terms of the insurance contract, which provides evidence of the contract.

CERTIFICATE

An additional document incorporating elements of the contract, and without which the insurance is not legal.

CLAIMS FORM

A form setting out the grounds for a claim, so the company can decide whether it comes under the terms of the policy.

SCHEDULE

Within a given class of business (eg Life, Fire, Accident, Motor) each company issues standard policies, identical to each other, and divided into clearly defined sections.

COVER NOTE

It normally takes some time between a proposal and the exact definition of the policy by the underwriters; during this time, legally there can be no cover.

SUM ASSURED

In some forms of insurance, eg Life, there can be no indemnity as such, as the financial loss of life cannot be estimated. Therefore a sum is covered related not to damage sustained but directly to premium. This is the sum assured.

UPDATING

The increase in the sum covered by a policy by
(a) changing the schedule on an indemnity policy
(b) increasing the sum assured

Recall to screen the first draft of the 'Insurance Documents and Terminology' file and make the following amendments using the **insert** facility. Proof-read carefully and store on disk. Print out one copy.

INSURANCE DOCUMENTS AND TERMINOLOGY

leave 2 clear line spaces here →

PROPOSAL

A request to /the/ insurers to provide cover.

POLICY

A document set*t*ing out the terms of the insurance contract, which provides evidence of the contract.

CERTIFICATE   *used in Motor, Marine and Employer Liability insurance,*

An additional document/ incorporating elements of the contract, and without which the insurance is not legal.

CLAIMS FORM

A form setting out the grounds for a claim, so/ *that* the company can decide whether it comes under the terms of the policy.

SCHEDULE

Within a given class of business (eg Life, Fire, Accident, Motor) each company issues <u>standard</u> policies, identical to each other, and divided into clearly defined sections. *The schedule contains all the information which is peculiar to that individual risk.*

COVER NOTE

It normally takes some time between a proposal and the exact definition of the policy by the underwriters; during this time, legally there can be no cover. *This is supplied by the issue of a memorandum from the company which gives temporary legal cover.*

SUM ASSURED

In some forms of insurance, eg Life, there can be no indemnity as such, as the financial loss of life cannot be estimated. Therefore a sum is covered related not to damage sustained but directly to premium. This is the sum assured.

UPDATING

insert a clear line space please →

The increase in the sum covered by a policy by
(a) changing the schedule on an indemnity policy
(b) increasing the sum assured

Open a new document file and key in the following using margins of 1"/2.5 cm. Store on disk.

A Complete Beauty Day - including a relaxing sauna, sunbed, full body massage, manicure, shampoo and blow dry, facial and make-up.

A 4-week Health & Fitness Programme - this will be held each morning, 9 am - 1 pm, and will include gym exercises, swim, sauna, shower and sunbeds.

Practice from the paper

Recall the above file and make the following amendments. Store and print one copy.

/ to be held
Monday -
Wednesday,

A Complete Beauty Day - /including a relaxing sauna, sunbed, full body massage, manicure, shampoo and blow dry, facial and make-up/.,and diet lunch   /

                    and
A 4-week Health & Fitness Programme - this will be held each morning, 9 am - 1 pm, ∧and will include gym exercises, swim, sauna, shower and sunbeds. (followed by lunch,)   /

Check your success

Did you use the *dash* and *hyphen* correctly, ie one space either side of the dash and no space in the hyphenated words (make-up and 4-week)? ☐

In the first insertion did you leave a space either side of Monday and Wednesday (a dash)? ☐

Did you remember to insert the comma after 'lunch' in the second insertion? ☐

Did you leave space after the '9' and the '1' before keying in the 'am' and 'pm'? ☐

10 Deleting text

Editing or revising a document file by using the delete facility to delete characters, words, phrases, sentences, line-space and paragraphs within existing text

You have probably already learnt to delete using the **backspace** and **delete** keys if you have noticed an error while you have been keying-in text in the previous exercises. The backspace and delete keys delete the character before or at the current cursor position. Depending on your system, you will probably have other commands for deleting larger amounts of text, ie words, lines, sentences or paragraphs. The system will need to be told how much text to delete, either by highlighting the text to be deleted using the cursor arrow keys or by placing the cursor at the beginning and the end of the deletion. The text will disappear from the screen and the surrounding text will move to fill up the space, according to the command sequence you have used to tell the system to carry out the process. It is also possible to delete characters, words etc by **overtyping**. On some systems you will be required to go into an overtyping mode. This method is useful if you are *replacing deleted text* with text of the same length but if the text is longer than that which is to be deleted you will also need to use the **insert** facility.

Note: Unless you have a back-up copy, the deleted text is usually gone for good!

Examples

Single character

δ⟍   dele̷ting   deleting

Word

δ⟍   you may ~~may~~ want to delete   you may want to delete

Phrase (delete and replace with other text)

initial
The ~~original~~ reasons for   The initial reasons for
introducing office   introducing office
technology were often   technology were often
somewhat arbitrary   somewhat arbitrary

A study by the clerical union, APEX, estimates that more than one third of the UK workforce is employed in clerical, administrative, professional and managerial occupations. ~~Within manufacturing industry, 28% of employees are in these occupations.~~ Over 40% of UK office time is spent on routine information activities.

A study by the clerical union, APEX, estimates that more than one third of the UK workforce is employed in clerical, administrative, professional and managerial occupations. Over 40% of UK office time is spent on routine information activities.

Line space

Air Canada for Business

Air Canada will be offering a new and more comfortable international executive class service for the business person.

leave only 1 clear line space →

This involves the refurbishment of their Boeing 747 fleet to allow for new seats and greater storage overhead.

Air Canada for Business

Air Canada will be offering a new and more comfortable international executive class service for the business person.

This involves the refurbishment of their Boeing 747 fleet to allow for new seats and greater storage overhead.

The Sports Centre is a good venue for all types of events.

It has been successfully used for Dances, Discos, Wedding Receptions, Children's Parties as well as meetings, conferences and seminars.

All bookings for the Centre should be made through the Centre Office - charges vary as to the type and time of use.

The Sports Centre is a good venue for all types of events.

All bookings for the Centre should be made through the Centre Office - charges vary as to the type and time of use.

Test your competence

Open a new document file and key in the first draft of the following circular letter. (*Note:* Type the current year – do not type 19..) Save to disk and print one copy.

May 19..

Dear Member

19.. has been a challenging year for the Society. The stability of the investment markets which prevailed during recent years declined at the end of 19.. and, after market levels had stabilised following their sharp initial falls, returns have been much lower.

However, in most markets investment yields have continued to outpace inflation and we believe that current prospects are supportive of continued 'real' returns, above both current and expected rates of inflation.

Despite market changes, we have been able to announce a substantial bonus which we believe to be very fair and attractive to all our without-profits policyholders.

As you know, we are a Mutual Society. We pay no dividends to shareholders and are thus able to pass on all our available profits to our qualifying policyholders.

I enclose a Member's Report which provides details of the bonus and indicates the Society's results for 19... I hope you will find this interesting.

Yours sincerely

Recall the last document file you keyed in (on page 33) and make the following amendments. Save to disk and print out one copy of the final version.

May 19..

Dear Member

19.. has been a challenging year for the Society. The buoyancy ~~stability~~ of the investment markets which prevailed during recent years declined at the end of 19.. and, ~~after market levels had stabilised following their sharp initial falls,~~ returns have been much lower.

However, in most markets investment yields have continued to outpace inflation and we believe that current prospects are supportive of continued 'real' returns, above both current and expected rates of inflation.

Despite market changes, we have been able to ~~announce~~ declare a substantial bonus which we believe to be ~~very~~ fair and attractive to all our with~~out~~-profits policyholders.

As you know, we are a Mutual Society. We pay no dividends to shareholders and are thus able to pass on all our available profits to ~~our~~ qualifying policyholders.

I enclose a Member's Report which provides details of the bonus and indicates the Society's results for 19... I hope you will find this of interest~~ing~~.

Yours sincerely

Open a new document file and key in the following text. Please copy *exactly* the layout, line spacing, use of upper and lower case characters, spacing and punctuation. It is *NOT* essential that line endings should be identical. Save to disk and print out one copy.

STEP ON IT

The harder you press the foot pedal, the quicker you go. Take it easy at first and when you want to stop just take your foot off the pedal. Practise on a spare piece of material first - you can control every stitch if you are careful.

TURNING CORNERS

Slow down as you approach the corner, and stop with the needle in the fabric. Lift the presser foot, swivel the material round to the new direction, and lower the foot again. You can now carry on stitching.

Recall the first draft of the extract from an article about sewing machines and carry out the revisions indicated below.
File the second draft and print out one copy.

STEP ON IT

The harder you press the foot pedal, the ~~quicker~~ *faster* you go. ⌐
Take it easy at first and when you want to stop just take
your foot off the pedal. Practise on a spare piece of
material first ~~- you can control every stitch if you are~~ ⌐
~~careful~~.
~~TURNING~~ *TAKING* CORNERS ⌐

Slow down as you approach the corner, and stop with the
needle in the fabric. Lift the presser foot, swivel the
material round ~~to the new direction~~, and lower the foot ⌐
again. You can now carry on stitching.

Check your success

Did you follow the instructions given to copy *exactly* the layout, line spacing, use of upper and lower case characters, spacing and punctuation? ☐

Did you successfully replace longer words with shorter ones
eg faster instead of quicker?
TAKING instead of TURNING? ☐

When deleting '... you can control every stitch if you are careful', did you retain the full stop at the end of the sentence? ☐

When deleting 'to the new direction', did you retain the comma? ☐

Practice from the paper

If you still have the exercise on disk that you keyed in on page 9, recall it and turn to page 36. Otherwise, open a new document file and key in the following. Please copy *exactly* the layout, line spacing, use of upper and lower case characters, spacing and punctuation. It is not essential that line endings should be identical. Save to disk and print out one copy.

Well Green Golf Club has enjoyed a culture of courtesy and
friendship since its inception, and expects a high standard
of behaviour both on and off the course.

Proposers of new members have a responsibility under the
Constitution of the Club to ensure that they are properly
introduced to the game and to the Club. On joining the
Club, all new members are expected to familiarise
themselves with the etiquette of play, as specified in the
Rules of Golf, and to observe these on the course.

Club staff are expected to behave courteously to members at
all times, as are members to them. On no account may a
member instruct or reprimand a member of staff directly.

Recall the extract from the Club Rules and carry out the revisions indicated below.
File your revised document and print out one copy.

Well Green Golf Club has enjoyed a ~~culture~~ *tradition* of courtesy and
friendship since its inception, and expects a high standard
of behaviour/both on and off the course.
  from members
Proposers of new members have a responsibility under the
Constitution of the Club to ensure that they are properly
introduced to the game and to the Club. On joining ~~the~~
~~Club~~, all new members are expected to familiarise
themselves with the etiquette of play, as specified in the
Rules of Golf, and to observe these on the course.

Club staff are expected to behave courteously to members at
all times, as are members to them. ~~On no account may a~~
~~member instruct or reprimand a member of staff directly.~~

Check your success   Did you follow instructions to copy *exactly* the layout, line spacing, use of upper
and lower case characters (eg Green Golf Club), spacing and punctuation?   ☐

Did you replace 'culture' with 'tradition'?   ☐

Did you make the text insertion in the first paragraph?   ☐

When deleting 'the Club', did you retain the comma?   ☐

Did you delete the final sentence?   ☐

11 Joining and splitting paragraphs

Editing or revising a document file by joining or splitting paragraphs

Joining or running on two paragraphs of text is usually carried out by removing or **deleting** the space between the two paragraphs. The cursor is usually positioned at the point at which the **join** is required (remember to leave two spaces after the full stop at the end of a sentence) and then the command sequence is given to delete the blank line between the paragraphs and any additional space.

Splitting text is carried out by inserting space. The cursor is positioned at the point at which the **split** is to occur and the command sequence is given to insert space, allowing for the extra clear line required between paragraphs.

With some systems it may also be necessary to reform or adjust the text after the operation.

Examples

Joining text

Run on

From medieval times, Wilton has been a prosperous weaving
centre.

It became the birthplace of significant carpet manufacture
in Britain in 1655, making Wilton Royal the oldest carpet
factory in the world that is still in production at its
original location.

From medieval times, Wilton has been a prosperous weaving
centre. It became the birthplace of significant carpet
manufacture in Britain in 1655, making Wilton Royal the
oldest carpet factory in the world that is still in production
at its original location.

N P

From medieval times, Wilton has been a prosperous weaving centre. [It became the birthplace of significant carpet manufacture in Britain in 1655, making Wilton Royal the oldest carpet factory in the world that is still in production at its original location.

From medieval times, Wilton has been a prosperous weaving centre.

It became the birthplace of significant carpet manufacture in Britain in 1655, making Wilton Royal the oldest carpet factory in the world that is still in production at its original location.

Test your competence

Open a new document file and key in the first draft of the following instructions regarding 'Customer Care'. Save to disk and print out one copy.

WHEN OUR CUSTOMERS TELEPHONE

Always ensure that telephones are answered promptly. Identify the company and department and, if appropriate, try to introduce your name to the caller early in the conversation. Speak with a 'smile in your voice' - a friendly, helpful approach is infectious.

Be businesslike, remembering to listen carefully, making notes as you go along. Ask positive questions and check back important details such as order number, delivery address and date required. Don't forget to offer linked items to the sale, and to thank the caller for the order or enquiry.

Noting the customer's telephone number when goods have been ordered is a useful safeguard.

Recall the above file and make the following amendments. Store to disk and print out one copy.

WHEN OUR CUSTOMERS TELEPHONE

NP

Always ensure that telephones are answered promptly. Identify the company and department and, if appropriate, try to introduce your name to the caller early in the conversation. [Speak with a 'smile in your voice' – a friendly, helpful approach is infectious.

run on

Be businesslike, remembering to listen carefully, making notes as you go along. Ask positive questions and check back important details such as order number, delivery address and date required. [Don't forget to offer linked items to the sale, and to thank the caller for the order or enquiry.

run on

Noting the customer's telephone number when goods have been ordered is a useful safeguard.

Practice from the paper

Open a new document file and key in the following text. Please copy the *exact* layout, line spacing, use of upper and lower case characters, spacing and punctuation. It is *not* essential that line endings should be identical. File your completed document and print out one copy.

The heavy frost, snow, gales and torrential rain has brought most outdoor gardening to a halt in recent weeks. The ground is not fit for planting and sowing.

It is going to take a long spell of sun and drying winds to make the top soil fit to walk upon – and to work.

Recall the above file and carry out the revisions indicated. File to disk and print out one copy.

have

The heavy frost, snow, gales and torrential rain has brought most outdoor gardening to a halt in recent weeks.

NP [The ground is not fit for planting and sowing / and

run on lc It is going to take a long spell of sun and drying winds to make the top soil fit to walk upon – and to work.

Check your success   When splitting the text did you leave a *clear line space* between the paragraphs?   ☐

When joining the text did you delete the full stop, add 'and' and make the 'I' lower   ☐
case?

Did you remember to make the other amendments,   ☐
ie delete the *comma* after 'snow';
    delete *gales*;
    delete *has* and replace with *have*?

12   Moving text

Edit or revise a document file by using the move facility to move text within a single document

Moving blocks of text is often referred to as cutting and pasting. When you *cut out* the text you also remove the space taken up by the text, ie the other text moves up and fills the gap. When you *paste in* the removed text you position the cursor at the *point of insertion* and then *insert* the text.

Most systems require you to identify the *block of text* to be *moved*. Markers can be made at the beginning and end of the block or an instruction given defining the amount of text (sentence, paragraph, remainder). Having identified the text, you will give an instruction to place the text in a temporary or buffer memory. You can then position the cursor at the required location and give the command to retrieve the text from the buffer memory. The text is then inserted and the surrounding text will move to allow for this insertion.

Example

WHEN OUR CUSTOMERS VISIT

Face to face selling is an enjoyable experience when the customer is friendly and easy going. Experience tells us that this is not always the case.

Counter Sales is the 'show business' of our industry. We all know that whatever the audience reaction, the show must go on - customers must leave our depots satisfied with the service.

We rely on your professionalism to handle awkward customers as politely and efficiently as the good ones.

WHEN OUR CUSTOMERS VISIT

Face to face selling is an enjoyable experience when the customer is friendly and easy going. Experience tells us that this is not always the case.

We rely on your professionalism to handle awkward customers as politely and efficiently as the good ones.

Counter Sales is the 'show business' of our industry. We all know that whatever the audience reaction, the show must go on - customers must leave our depots satisfied with the service.

Open a new document file and key in the first draft of the following text. Save to disk and print out one copy.

Dear Guest

Channelink British Ferries are delighted that you have been able to join this trip to visit Normandy and to see what services we offer on board our ships.

We arrive in Cherbourg tomorrow morning at 0615 hours local time. You will therefore be pleased to learn that this evening's briefing session will be kept as short as possible.

Tomorrow we will be making a whistle-stop tour of many of the tourist attractions and natural delights of Normandy. The pace will be fairly brisk, so be sure to get some shuteye now and enjoy tomorrow.

We hope that you find everything to your satisfaction on board the M V Nelson. If there is anything you require and if this is not provided, then please let any of the Channelink representatives with the party know so that we can rectify the matter.

WELCOME ABOARD

Test your competence

Recall the above draft letter and make the following amendments. Store to disk and print out one copy of the final version.

Dear Guest

Channelink British Ferries are delighted that you have been able to join this trip to visit Normandy and to see what services we offer on board our ships.

We arrive in Cherbourg tomorrow morning at 0615 hours local time. You will therefore be pleased to learn that this evening's briefing session will be kept as short as possible.

Tomorrow we will be making a whistle-stop tour of many of the tourist attractions and natural delights of Normandy. The pace will be fairly brisk, so be sure to get some shuteye now and enjoy tomorrow.

We hope that you find everything to your satisfaction on board the M V Nelson. If there is anything you require and if this is not provided, then please let any of the Channelink representatives with the party know so that we can rectify the matter.

WELCOME ABOARD

Practice from the paper

Open a new document file and key in the following.

Please copy *exactly* the layout, line spacing, use of upper and lower case characters, spacing and punctuation. It is *not* essential that line endings should be identical.

File your completed document and print out one copy.

CLOCHES

You may soon be able to sow the first vegetable seeds under cloches. Sow peas as soon as possible in a drill down the centre, and put in a few radish seeds and lettuce down the outside edge.

Although cloches are an expensive item, they do give a good yield of extra vegetables and salad ingredients.

If the ground is still unworkable, try bringing on some plants under glass or on a sunny windowsill before planting out in the cloches. This will give them a head start while you are waiting for the ground to be ready.

Practice from the paper

Recall the above file and carry out the revisions as indicated. File the second version and print out one copy.

CLOCHES

Feltham First ⋏   You may soon be able to sow the first vegetable seeds under cloches. Sow peas as soon as possible in a drill down the centre, and put in a few radish seeds and lettuce down the outside edge.   *Little Gem* ⋏

�⌐ Although cloches are ~~an~~ expensive ~~item~~, they do give a good yield of extra vegetables and salad ingredients.

If the ground is still unworkable, try bringing on some plants under glass or on a sunny windowsill before planting out in the cloches. This will give them a head start while you are waiting for the ground to be ready.

Check your success

Did you carry out the move successfully? ☐

Did you delete the 'an' and 'item' within the paragraph to be moved? ☐

Did you insert 'Feltham First' and 'Little Gem' correctly? ☐

Did you proof-read carefully? ☐

13 Presenting documents in an acceptable style

Present in a correct and acceptable form standard business documents from handwritten or typewritten drafts using a currently acceptable style of presentation of paragraphs, punctuation, spacing, material in columns, the dash/hyphen key (*see* page 279). Respond to printers' correction signs

In the examination you will be required to key in a business document from either a *handwritten* or *typewritten* draft. The draft will probably contain amendments in the form of printers' correction signs.

When copying from the draft it is important to key in the text exactly as it appears on the examination copy, with the exception of line endings. For example, do not change blocked paragraphs to indented paragraphs unless requested to do so.

Test your competence

The following exercises will ensure that you practise different *examples* of office correspondence.

Business letter

Open a new document file and key in the following letter. Respond to the author's instructions and use of printers' correction signs. Save to disk and print one copy.

Nairobi Audio Visual Services
Kenyatta Place
NAIROBI
Tel: 364239

(Today's date)

Dear Customer

SPECIAL OFFERS

We are able to offer

⌐ ~~As one~~ of our long standing clients an extremely

⌐ favourable and competitive price ~~for~~ deals on 2 of our

current models.

⌐ The NAVS 140 14" colour TV with Remote Control and

built-in timer and 30 channel presets is on offer at

u/s   *only* 10,000 shillings.

The NAVS 1585 21" has FST (flatter squarer tube)
technology for a superb picture /and less reflection.
with a wider viewing angle

u/s   On offer at *only* 15,000 shillings.

If you are interested in viewing either of the above
models please call in at our showroom as soon as
possible.

Yours faithfully

B Osogo
Manager

Advertisement   Open a new document file and key in the following advertisement. Respond to the author's instructions and use of printers' correction signs. Save to disk and print one copy.

Nairobi Audio Visual Services
K Jenyatta Place
NAIROBI
Tel: 364239

Monday – Friday   8.00 – 13.00

WE'RE HERE !

If you are looking for a
T.V. or VIDEO RECORDER

LOOK NO FURTHER . . .

Centre each line

We offer
    Numerous Products
    At Keen Prices
    Very good Customer Relations
    Superb Audio/Visual Products

Centre each line

Open a new document file and key in the following memo. Respond to the author's instructions and use of printers' correction signs. Remember to type today's date. Save to disk and print one copy.

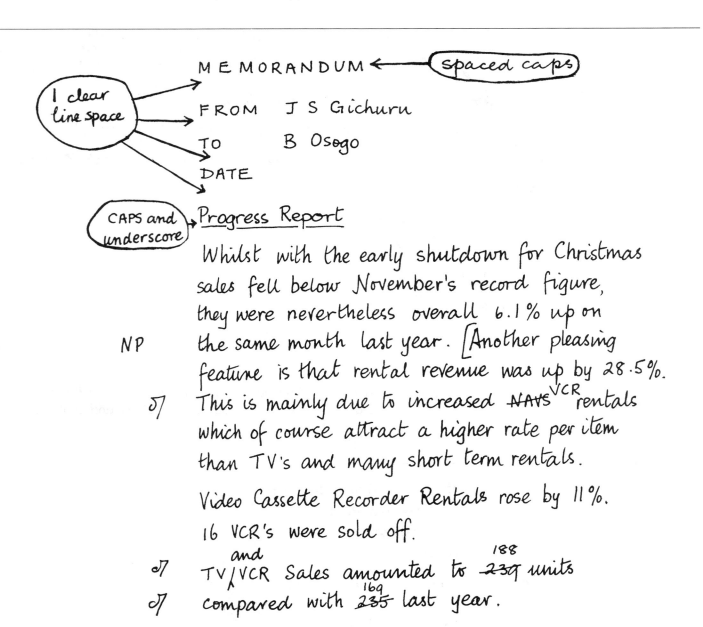

M E M O R A N D U M ← (spaced caps)

(1 clear line space)

FROM   J S Gichuru

TO   B Osogo

DATE

(CAPS and underscore) → Progress Report

Whilst with the early shutdown for Christmas sales fell below November's record figure, they were nevertheless overall 6.1% up on the same month last year. [Another pleasing feature is that rental revenue was up by 28.5%.

NP

This is mainly due to increased ~~NAVS~~ VCR rentals which of course attract a higher rate per item than TV's and many short term rentals.

Video Cassette Recorder Rentals rose by 11%.

16 VCR's were sold off.

and
TV/VCR Sales amounted to ~~239~~ 188 units

compared with ~~235~~ 169 last year.

Caps and underscore | E for Ecology

This is the throwaway age. Almost everything that we purchase comes wrapped in plastic, is bottled, boxed or canned. This packaging costs a great deal. It uses up our raw materials. For example trees are used to make cardboard, oil is used to make plastic. [Indeed, every time you go and do your weekly shop in the local supermarket there is about £5 worth of packaging in your trolley.

NP
¶

When you eventually get home with all those goodies and unpack them you are contributing to the 14 million tonnes of waste disposed of each year!

stet

Admittedly, some of the paper waste will rot away – it's biodegradable. Glass and most plastics are non-biodegradable and if burnt produce deadly gases.

trs
¶

What can we do?

u/s

The solution is to produce _less_ waste. We should use less packaging, use returnable, refillable and re-usable containers. Only biodegradable, recyclable packaging should be used.

u/s
u/s

Key in the following document. Please use the layout, spacing, etc, as indicated. File your completed document and print out one copy.

---

caps and underscore → <u>The Golden Girl Health Centre</u> is pleased to be able to offer the following:

<u>IONITHERMIE</u>

and effective ⟋ This is a revolutionary new/treatment for Cellulite, which has been widely and favourably publicised in the national press.

Most women suffer from having fat deposits on certain parts of the body, and any amount of dieting will not

stet ~~bring about~~ the required reduction of those particular areas. Re-shaping of the figure is required - not general weight-loss. This new Cellulite treatment gives a greater degree of control over figure shaping than dieting can, and the manufacturers claim that the treatment also rejuvenates the skin.

¶ Many women suffer embarrassment from unsightly fat deposits at some time in their lives - particularly after child-birth or in 'middle age'. This can cause anxiety and lead to a state of severe depression.

If you would like to take advantage of our introductory offer of 10% off the cost of a course of this treatment, ring for a free consultation (Milton Keynes 650299).

<u>IONITHERMIE</u> is designed to make you look and feel more beautiful - more feminine.

Check your success

Did you change the first *paragraph heading* to capital letters? ☐

Did you underscore both the words and spaces between? ☐

Did you make the text insertion? ☐

Did you *retain* the words with the dotted line underneath? ☐

Did you *miss out* the paragraph with the deletion mark? ☐

Did you make correct use of the *dash* between 'required – not' and 'beautiful – more'? ☐

Did you *hyphenate* 'Re-shaping' and 'weight-loss'? ☐

Open a new document file and key in the following. Please copy *exactly* the layout, line spacing, use of upper and lower case characters, spacing and punctuation. It is *not* essential that the line endings should be identical.

File your completed document and print out one copy.

P R O G R A M M E   N O T E S

SYMPHONY NO 5 IN E MINOR
Opus 64

                                        Peter Ilyich Tchaikovsky
                                        (1840-1893)

Andante - allegro con anima
Adante cantabile, con alcuna licenza
Allegro moderato
Andante maestoso - allegro vivace

In view of the great popularity of his major works today, it
is difficult to comprehend Tchaikovsky's deep sense of
inadequacy regarding his own worth as a composer.

He was at his happiest in 1885, when he moved into a country
house where he was able to relax between regular tours abroad.
His reputation was growing, and to his surprise he found himself increasingly in demand on the rostrum, where in his earlier
years he had felt such a failure.

Now he was able to travel, meet other composers, and then return
to the solitude of the country to work. But even throughout the
creation of his Fifth Symphony his letters still alternated
between joy and despair. Writing to his brother, Modeste, he
tells of how he is working on the symphony slowly and laboriously,
and of his determination to prove not only to others but also to
himself that he is not yet played out.

Check your success

Did you leave 3 spaces between the words in the heading in *spaced caps*? ☐

Did you use *closed caps* for the first line of the next heading? ☐

Did you calculate the position of Peter Ilyich Tchaikovsky so that the 'y' ended at the ☐
right-hand margin?

Did you type his name accurately? ☐

Did you follow the copy and leave *no* space each side of the hyphen between 1840 ☐
and 1893?

Did you leave space either side of the dashes? ☐

Did you follow the *spacing* between headings and paragraphs as given? ☐

Did you proof-read carefully? ☐

14 Inserting variable information

Recall a standard document from disk and create a final document by keying in variable information at in-fill points

In the examination the lecturer or tutor will have previously set up the *standard document* on disk with appropriate symbols (eg & or $) or bracketed numbers (1) at the **in-fill** points (see the example below). You will be required to recall the file and, using the **search** or **find** facility (or the cursor control keys), find the correct position in the document for the insertion of the **variable information**. It is advisable to take a *copy* of the standard document and call this to screen so that the *original version* is intact. This would be the procedure adopted if several documents were to be created using the *standard* document as a base, **personalising** each version by inserting the *different* variable information each time.

Always take care to position the cursor at the point of the *in-fill* and to insert the required information correctly. You must delete or type over the *symbols or bracketed numbers*.

If the document requires a date then this must be presented in a recognised and acceptable form, eg:

7 June 1990 or 7th June 1990

It is equally important *not* to delete any of the *standard document* (apart from the symbols or bracketed numbers mentioned above).

Note: This is not a merge task. The variables are inserted manually.

Examples
Standard document with in-fill points

```
Ref:   785432/AP

$

$

Dear $

Thank you for your completed booking form and deposit.
Please find enclosed the confirmation and account for your
holiday in $, departing on $.

Would you please let us have your remittance for $ to cover
the balance of your account by $ at the latest.

Yours sincerely
TRAVELLERS WORLD



Martin Armstrong

Enc
```

The instructions to the candidate will present the variable information in handwritten or typed form, indicating which insertion is to be made at each point.

In the example below the variables have been underlined.

```
Ref:   785432/AP

7 June 19..   (you are often asked to insert today's date)

Miss Yoko Ikema
128 Gloucester Road
CHELTENHAM
Glos
GL50 3DU

Dear Miss Ikema

Thank you for your completed booking form and deposit.
Please find enclosed the confirmation and account for your
holiday in Egypt, departing on 17 March.

Would you please let us have your remittance for £387.50 to
cover the balance of your account by 12 July at the latest.

Yours sincerely
TRAVELLERS WORLD



Martin Armstrong

Enc
```

Open a new document file and set up the following standard document. Use the appropriate symbols or *stop codes* at the points indicated. Save to disk.

Some systems allow the setting up of *stop codes*, which are *find* marks that take the cursor automatically from one mark to another. Depending on your system, this may be quicker and more accurate than using the cursor.

MW/AP

(1)

(2)

Dear (3)

Thank you for your order No (4) which was received today.

In accordance with your instructions we have reserved (5) in the issues of (6) inclusive, and confirm that the cost per insertion will be (7) shillings.

May we remind you that copy is required 4 weeks prior to date of publication.

Yours sincerely
NAIROBI JOURNAL

D Ndola
Advertising Department

Recall the standard letter and insert the items listed below in the appropriate places. Please note that the numbers in brackets are there to indicate where the insertions are to be made, and should *not* appear in the finished document.

Please use today's date. Save to disk and print one copy.

---

(1) (today's date)

(2) Mr R Roberts
IPS Building
Kimathi Street
NAIROBI

(3) Richard

(4) A4792

(5) 4 half pages

(6) March to June

(7) 94

Set up the following standard letter on disk using appropriate symbols or codes at the in-fill points. Save to disk.

KK/dw

(1)

(2)

Dear (3)

Thank you for renewing your subscription to the TUNEWELL ORCHESTRA CLUB.

Advance booking for the Opening Concert of the new season at the (4) Hall on (5) opens on (6), and your priority booking form is enclosed. If you would like to attend, you are asked to apply for your free pass by (7) at the latest.

Your student card is returned herewith.

I look forward to meeting you at the Members' Reception before the Opening Concert.

Yours sincerely

Membership Secretary

Enc

A standard letter has been prepared and filed on the storage medium. Recall it, and insert the items listed below in the appropriate places. Please use today's date. File your completed document and print out one copy.

(1) (Today's date)

(2) Mr James Morgan
    49 High Street
    CANTERING

(3) Mr Morgan

(4) Royal Festival

(5) 4 October

(6) 23 August

(7) 13 September

Check your success

Did you present the date in an acceptable style? ☐

Did you retain the *open punctuation* used in the copy for the addressee? ☐

Did you consistently use *open punctuation* throughout the task? ☐

Did you remove the bracketed numbers successfully? ☐

Did you make the insertions at the correct location? ☐

Did you proof-read your insertions to check for accuracy? ☐

15 Proof-reading on screen and against copy

Proof-read on screen a document containing obvious keying in errors of grammatical agreement, punctuation and display, and recognise and correct errors
Proof-read against copy a document that you have recalled or edited and recognise and correct errors

In carrying out the previous exercises you have been learning to be more competent at proof-reading on screen, either from creating a document or from making amendments to an existing document. These are called *running corrections*.

You may find that proof-reading from the screen is more difficult than identifying errors in a printout or *hard copy*. In addition to identifying errors on the screen, it is also necessary to check that the information lines, eg the status and ruler lines, are accurate. You may need to ask yourself the following questions: Is the margin correct? Are tabs set appropriately? Is the line spacing correct?

You should also be familiar with the **screen symbols** used by your particular system. Most systems have symbols to indicate that a *hard carriage return* has been made at the end of headings and paragraphs. This is often shaped like a triangle on its side. If you do not allow the text to wrap at line endings and instead press the carriage return key, then the screen symbols will indicate this. It would then be time-consuming to edit the text as only one line of text can be reformed at a time. Some systems use **embedded commands** to carry out such functions as underscoring and emboldening text. These are visual symbols on the screen which indicate that underscoring or emboldening will occur at *printout* stage (for example WordStar's ^S). It is important to check that these commands are correct and that they tell the system *when to start* and *when to stop*. Every time you use the spacebar, this creates what is called a *hard space*. Every word should have a space after it. The punctuation marks at the end of the sentences, eg full stops, question marks and exclamation marks, should all have at least one space after them. It is common practice to leave two spaces. Either method is correct *but* you must be consistent.

When checking text that has been keyed in using a *ragged right margin* (uneven or irregular) it is important to check that the text has been **reformed** or redesigned so that it fits into the set margins. Some systems require you to give a reform command after making alterations by *inserting* or *deleting* text. If this is not carried out, then the text extends beyond the fixed right-hand margin and you will be penalised.

Proof-reading involves looking for the differences between two versions of a document. As a child you probably enjoyed 'spot the difference' competitions in which you had to find a certain number of differences between two pictures. Looking for differences in typed or written work is perhaps more difficult. However, with practice, you can be *trained* to develop this essential skill.

It is obviously important to locate and correct errors in work produced on a word processor, especially if the final document, for example, a report, is going to be printed out in multiple copies — thus multiplying the number of times the error is reproduced!

Many different kinds of error can be made. These include simple keyboarding errors, spelling mistakes, words or phrases omitted or inserted in the wrong place, words keyed in the wrong way round (transposed), missing apostrophes, incorrect line spacing between paragraphs or headings, etc. In addition you will also need to check for

inconsistency in the use of style of layout, eg a combination of open and closed punctuation or blocked and indented paragraphs.

In the examination the screen document containing the errors will have been keyed in by your lecturer or tutor prior to the examination. You will be required to recall the screen document and check it against the correct copy which will be given to you. You will be asked to *amend* all the errors, store the new version to disk and print out a version.

Not only are you required to locate and correct the errors but you must ensure that you do not make *additional* errors by altering existing text which is *accurate*.

Example
Screen version (containing errors)

```
Kinstone
PO Box 70397          — transpose
Ndola
ZAMBIA

Dear Mr Matala          — overtype 'o'

            insert space        delete letter      delete extra
                                     delete space        letter
Thank you for your recent enquirey regarding our forthcomming
Sales Development and Training Seminar. The leader of the       insert
Seminar is Joseph Peterson, whose sales management and training   comma
experience is extensive and spans over 25 years, mainly in Europe,
Australia, North America and Africa.                    delete extra
                                                              word
Change   I am sure that you will be particularly interested in in the
to u.c.  Seminar entitled 'Writing Sales Letters and Proposals that Sell'.  insert 'r'
         This is a practical Seminar where delegates will learn the corect
overtype ways of writing sales letters and will look in detail at the
'w'      structure for writing sales proposals that are persasive and that  insert 'u'
transpose really sell.  Delegates will be able analyse their own existing  insert 'to'
letters  written proposals and quotations, and be given the opportunity to
         improve and re-write them following the Guidelines been discussed.
            delete        delete                    change    alter to 'being'
            Space         hyphen                     to l.c.
delete
'e'
```

Correct copy

```
Kinstone
PO Box 70937
Ndola
ZAMBIA

Dear Mr Matalo

Thank you for your recent enquiry regarding our forthcoming
Sales Development and Training Seminar.  The leader of the
Seminar is Joseph Peterson, whose sales, management and training
experience is extensive and spans over 25 years, mainly in Europe,
Australia, North America and Africa.

I am sure that you will be particularly interested in the
Seminar entitled 'Writing Sales Letters and Proposals that Sell'.
This is a practical Seminar where delegates will learn the correct
ways of writing sales letters and will look in detail at the
structure for writing sales proposals that are persuasive and
that really sell.  Delegates will be able to analyse their own
existing written proposals and quotations, and be given the
opportunity to improve and rewrite them following the guidelines
being discussed.
```

Please key in the proof-reading task below. Care should be taken to ensure that all the errors are repeated when this document is created. To help in your preparation, check with page 59 where the *deliberate mistakes* are circled. Save to disk.

Note: If it is *not* possible for the tutor/lecturer to set up this task on disk to make it more realistic, turn to page 58.

CONTRACT OF EMPLOYMENT

THIS CONTRACT OF EMPLOYMENT is made the FIFTENTH day of DECEMBER 19..

BETWEEN

(A) THE GOLDEN GIRL HEALTH CENTRE, The Boulevard, Milton Keynes, Bucks (the Employer) and

(B   John Mitchell, 1 Oak Lane, Bletchley, (the Employee)

1   THIS Agreement is pursuant made to the Contracts of Employment Act 1972 S4

2   THE Employee's employment began and the terms of the employment applied on the date hereof
3   THE Employee is employed as Beauty Consultent at weekly wage of £85.00
4   THE Employee's hours of work is 9 am – 7 pm Monday to Wednesday, 9 am – 5 pm Thursday and Friday, and 9 am – 1 pm Saturday, with morning and aftertoon tea breaks of 15 minutes and one hour for for lunch

5   THE Employee is entitled to 15 days' holiday with pay in addition to the Bank Holidays

6   THERE is no Pension Scheme in existence

7   THE employee will not be entitled to any wages for absance longer than 3 hours 20 minutes in any day for sickness or injuries

8. The Employee is entitled to four weeks' notice and may give two weeks' notice to terminate her employment.

SIGNED on behalf of the Employer   ....
in the presence of

                                             ....

signed by   ....
in the presence of

                                             ....

Recall the previous file to screen. Carefully proof-read the document, checking against the *perfect copy* below. Correct **all errors**, file the revised version and print out one copy.

Note: If this task has not been keyed in already by your tutor or lecturer, proof-read the incorrect copy on the previous page against the copy below.

<u>CONTRACT OF EMPLOYMENT</u>

THIS CONTRACT OF EMPLOYMENT is made the FIFTEENTH day of DECEMBER 19..

BETWEEN

(A)   THE GOLDEN GIRL HEALTH CENTRE, The Boulevard, Milton Keynes, Bucks (the Employer) and

(B)   Janet Mitchell, 1 Oak Lane, Bletchley, Bucks (the Employee)

1   THIS Agreement is made pursuant to the Contracts of Employment Act 1972 S 4

2   THE Employee's employment began and the terms of the employment applied on the date hereof

3   THE Employee is employed as Beauty Consultant at the weekly wage of £85.00

4   THE Employee's hours of work are 9 am - 7 pm Monday to Wednesday, 9 am - 5 pm Thursday and Friday, and 9 am - 1 pm Saturday, with morning and afternoon tea breaks of 15 minutes and one hour for lunch

5   THE Employee is entitled to 15 days' holiday with pay in addition to the Bank Holidays

6   THERE is no Pension Scheme in existence

7   THE Employee will not be entitled to any wages for absence longer than 3 hours 30 minutes in any day for sickness or injuries

8   THE Employee is entitled to four weeks' notice and may give two weeks' notice to terminate her employment

SIGNED on behalf of the Employer   ....
in the presence of
                                          ....

SIGNED by   ....
in the presence of
                                          ....

CONTRACT OF EMPLOYMENT

THIS CONTRACT OF EMPLOYMENT is made the FIFTENTH day of DECEMBER 19..

BETWEEN

(A)   THE GOLDEN GIRL HEALTH CENTRE, The Boulevard, Milton Keynes, Bucks (the Employer) and

(B)   John Mitchell, 1 Oak Lane, Bletchley, ⬭ (the Employee)

1   THIS Agreement is pursuant made to the Contracts of Employment Act 1972 S4

2   THE Employee's employment began and the terms of the employment applied on the date hereof

3   THE Employee is employed as Beauty Consultent at weekly wage of £85.00

4   THE Employee's hours of work is 9 am - 7 pm Monday to Wednesday, 9 am - 5 pm Thursday and Friday, and 9 am - 1 pm Saturday, with morning and aftertoon tea breaks of 15 minutes and one hour for for lunch

5   THE Employee is entitled to 15 days' holiday with pay in addition to the Bank Holidays

6   THERE is no Pension Scheme in existence

7   THE employee will not be entitled to any wages for absance longer than 3 hours 20 minutes in any day for sickness or injuries

8. The Employee is entitled to four weeks' notice and may give two weeks' notice to terminate her employment.

SIGNED on behalf of the Employer   ....
in the presence of

                                          ....

signed by   ....
in the presence of

                                          ....

Please key in the proof-reading task below. Care should be taken to ensure that all the errors are repeated when this document is created. To help in your preparation, check with page 61 where the *deliberate mistakes* are circled. Save to disk.

Note: If it is *not* possible for the tutor/lecturer to set up this task on disk to make it more realistic, proof-read the incorrect copy below against the corrected copy which follows it.

```
Tschaikovsky's Fifth Synphony is dominated by a motto them
which open the work, features in the two central
movements, and with all the confidence of the major key,
becomes the main theme of the finale.

The Andante introduction tothe first movement start with
the steme played by clarients in their lowest register,
contrasted with slow, deliverate steps by the strings.
With the commencement of the allegro, the motto takes over
as the main theme, contrasting with the second subject, a
gentle waltz tune from the violins, which provides a relive
from the prevailing mood of pessimism

At first the andante cantabile transports the listener into
a romantic world of serene charm.  The horn melody of the
opening, and and the oboe tune of the second theme are
Tchaikovsky at his melodic best.  But the calm are
deceptive, for twice the motto theme enters  ominously.
The delightful waltz of the third mvoement is followed by
a sininister reappearance of the motto at the end.  Yet
the finale opens with a transformation of the theme into
the major, almost in the character of a hymn.  The allegro
vivace introduces a strong dramatic theme, the march-like
background grows in excitement, and the music rises to a
triumphant climax in blaze of color and glory.
```

**Practice from the
paper**

Programme Notes for Tchaikovsky's Fifth Symphony have been rough drafted on the word processor (previous document file), and you have been asked to proof-read the text and make all the necessary corrections.

Recall the draft, and check it against the correct copy which appears below. Amend all errors, file your revised version of the document and print out one copy.

```
Tchaikovsky's Fifth Symphony is dominated by a motto theme
which opens the work, features in the two central
movements, and with all the confidence of the major key,
becomes the main theme of the finale.

The andante introduction to the first movement starts with
the theme played by clarinets in their lowest register,
contrasted with slow, deliberate steps by the strings.
With the commencement of the allegro, the motto takes over
as the main theme, contrasting with the second subject, a
gentle waltz tune from the violins, which provides a relief
from the prevailing mood of pessimism.

At first the andante cantabile transports the listener into
a romantic world of serene charm.  The horn melody of the
opening, and the oboe tune of the second theme are
Tchaikovsky at his melodic best.  But the calm is
deceptive, for twice the motto theme enters ominously.
The delightful waltz of the third movement is followed by
a sinister reappearance of the motto at the end.  Yet
the finale opens with a transformation of the theme into
the major, almost in the character of a hymn.  The allegro
vivace introduces a strong dramatic theme, the march-like
background grows in excitement, and the music rises to a
triumphant climax in a blaze of colour and glory.
```

Check your success The 'deliberate mistakes' have been circled to aid identification. Check carefully against your printout to make sure that you managed to correct them all.

(Tschaikovsky's) Fifth (Synphony) is dominated by a motto (them) which (open) the work, features in the two central movements, and with all the confidence of the major key, becomes the main theme of the finale.

The (Andante) introduction (tothe) first movement (start) with the (steme) played by (clarients) in their lowest register, contrasted with slow, (deliverate) steps by the strings. With the commencement of the allegro, the motto takes over as the main theme, contrasting with the second subject, a gentle waltz tune from the violins, which provides a (relive) from the prevailing mood of (pessimism)

At first the (andante cantabile) transports the listener into a romantic world of serene charm. The horn melody of the opening, (and and) the oboe tune of the second theme are Tchaikovsky at his melodic best. But the calm (are) deceptive, for twice the motto theme enters (O) ominously. The delightful waltz of the third (mvoement) is followed by a (sininister) reappearance of the motto at the end. Yet the finale opens with a transformation of the theme into the major, almost in the character of a hymn. The allegro vivace introduces a strong dramatic theme, the march-like background grows in excitement, and the music rises to a triumphant climax (in blaze) of (color) and glory.

How many different types of corrections were there? Check this using the list below.
Note: not all those listed necessarily appeared.

straight keyboarding errors (ie pressing incorrect key)   ☐

extra characters or words inserted   ☐

extra characters or words omitted   ☐

transposition of letters or words   ☐

underscore omitted   ☐

spacing errors   ☐

grammatical errors   ☐

punctuation errors   ☐

spelling errors   ☐

use of upper case instead of lower case   ☐

use of lower case instead of upper case   ☐

16   Elementary examination questions

There now follows an Elementary Examination paper, which has been worked through and solutions provided. It is suggested that you work through the paper before comparing your printout with the solutions.

Please note that these are model answers only and in no way do they carry the authority of the Examining Board.

However, in order to tackle the tasks in conditions which mirror examination conditions, it will be necessary for the **tutor** to follow the **Specialist Teacher's Instructions Sheet** in order to set up those tasks which need to be previously stored on disk.

Further practice

For further practice, copies of past papers can be obtained from PEI. It is suggested that you practise working through as many papers as possible before taking the examination.

Note: See **Section 35 Preparing for the Word Processing examinations** for further helpful hints.

This paper must be returned
with the candidates' work.
Failure to do so will result in
delay in processing the
candidates' scripts.

No.

PITMAN
EXAMINATIONS
INSTITUTE

This pack contains:

*One Specialist Teacher's Instructions
Sheet and details of the Tasks to be
created on the storage medium.*

One Instruction Sheet per candidate.

One Instruction Sheet for Invigilators.

One Question Paper per candidate.

SPECIALIST TEACHER'S INSTRUCTIONS

To be handed to the Specialist Teacher before the date of the examination,
together with the sheets "Instructions to Candidates". NO OTHER PART OF
THE EXAMINATION PAPER MAY BE HANDED TO THE SPECIALIST TEACHER.

1   In advance of the date of the examination, you are asked to create
     documents on the storage medium for the attached tasks.

2   You may use any acceptable typing pitch, eg 10, 12, 15 or proportional
     spacing, as long as this is suitable for the printer(s) to be used in the
     examination. However, you must use a page format which would result in a
     minimum left hand margin of 1" (2.5 cm).

3   With the exception of line endings, which may vary with the choice of
     pitch, please follow the text exactly (including "deliberate mistakes").
     However, at the Specialist Teacher's discretion infill points/stop codes
     may be inserted in the standard document, replacing, or in addition to,
     the bracketed numbers/letters.

4   Copies of these documents should be created on the storage medium for the
     exclusive use of each individual candidate.

5   Print out a copy of your work to be attached to the Attestation Form for
     the examination.

6   Because word processing systems vary so widely between Centres it is not
     possible for the Examiner to specify file names for documents. Please
     allocate suitable file names for the documents created (TASK 1, TASK 2,
     etc are suggested, as appropriate). Likewise, please devise suitable
     file names for candidates to store their completed tasks.

(continued overleaf)

7 Please complete the relevant spaces provided on the "Instructions to Candidates" sheet, so that these file names may be handed to candidates at the start of the examination. This must be completed by the Specialist Teacher before the examination. Under no circumstances may candidates complete this form.

8 The preparation of all examination material must be regarded as strictly confidential and should be carried out under the supervision of the Examinations Secretary. No details of the content of the examination may be divulged. This should be enclosed with the worked scripts, together with a printed specimen copy of each of the prepared tasks.

9 All material must be erased from the system and storage medium at the end of the examination after the completion of all the required printing.

Note: *Please complete the filename on the form on page 67.*

Specialist teacher to store on disk.

<u>TASK 3</u>   (Candidate's Name)

A meeting of the Committee of the Newtown Branch of the Textwell
Users' Association will be held in the Conference Room at (1) on (2).

A G E N D A

1   Apologies for absence

2   Minutes of last meeting

3   Matters arising from the minutes

4   Chairman's Report

5   Secretary's Report

6   Treasurer's Report

     (3)

     (4)

     (5)

     (6)

     Any other business

     Date of next meeting

(*leave 4 clear line spaces here*)

Mary Rogers
Branch Secretary

TECHNICAL FACTSHEET

Functions of the XS85 range from sohisticated networking and telecomunications applications to exisitng WP and document transfer. Features include the 32-bit architecture already found inthe XS 90 and XS 100; a disk storage capacity of of over five gigabytes; and support of 32 concurrent users, increasing to up to 48 concurrent users with the additionof the optional cashe memory which allows configuration of either a seocnd disk IOP or tape IOP, supporting up to eight disk derives.

The basic XS 85 includes 32-bit CPU with 1MB of main memory, expandable to up to 4MB; the ZS oeprating system; one language (Assembler); a 16-port serial IOP; a 48K archiving workstation and one compiler. A wide variety of disk storage devices are available with packeaged systems, starting with 90NB.

As a standalone system, the XS 85 offers remote workstation capabilties, mainfarme emulation, and local and/or remote networking. The system also addresses other OA functions, such as WP, docunent transfer, calendar faciltiies, graphics and a wide range of DP facilities. The use of all available XS periperals is possible, such as remote, archiving and audio workstations; the Personal Computer; the 6400 graphics workstation; matrix, daisy and band printers; tape and disk drives.

SPECIALIST TEACHER PLEASE NOTE

The above is a proof-reading task. To aid your preparation the "deliberate mistakes" are circled and care should be taken to ensure that errors are repeated when this document is created.

WORD PROCESSING - ELEMENTARY

No.

CANDIDATE'S NAME ....
(Block letters please)

CENTRE NO. ....DATE ....

INSTRUCTIONS TO CANDIDATES   PAPER NO: ....

1   Before starting each task, read carefully the instructions printed at the top of the page, and follow these exactly. You will be marked on your ability to follow instructions.

2   The task number should appear as indicated on the copy. At the top right-hand corner of each task you should delete the words "Candidate's Name" and insert your own name instead. This must be done before you store the document, and your name should appear at the top of every page.

3   The Invigilator will give you instructions about page format. With the exception of line endings, which may vary with the choice of pitch, YOU MUST FOLLOW CAREFULLY THE STYLE OF LAYOUT AND DISPLAY SHOWN ON THE PRINTED EXAMINATION PAPER.

4   For some of the tasks on this paper, documents have been prepared in advance and stored on the storage medium. Because word processing systems vary so widely between Centres, the Invigilator has been asked to give you instructions regarding the location of these documents (see list below).

TASK NO	DOCUMENT STORED AS	FILE YOUR DOCUMENT AS
1		
2		
3		
4		

© Sir Isaac Pitman Ltd 1991

WORD PROCESSING - ELEMENTARY

This paper must be returned with the candidate's work, otherwise the entry will be void and no result will be issued.

No

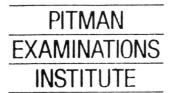

CANDIDATE'S NAME ....
(Block letters please)

CENTRE NO. ....DATE ....

This examination lasts for one hour, plus 5 minutes' reading time, and consists of four tasks which you should file on the storage medium for printing out later. The Invigilator will give you instructions about arrangements for printing out your documents.

YOU MUST ATTEMPT AND SUBMIT ALL FOUR TASKS.

FOR EXAMINER'S USE ONLY

COMPLETION	ACCURACY	DISPLAY

TASK 1

You are asked to key in the following document, following the Invigilator's instructions regarding format and margin settings.

Please copy <u>exactly</u> the layout, line spacing, use of upper and lower case characters, spacing and punctuation. It is <u>not</u> essential that line endings should be identical.

File your completed document for printing out later.

<u>TASK 1</u>   (Candidate's Name)

<u>DRAFT</u>

TEXTWELL USERS' NEWSLETTER - JANUARY EDITION

<u>Word Processing Problem Corner</u>

One of the benefits of membership of the Textwell Users'
Association is the opportunity to draw on the experience of fellow
members, and to share our own knowledge and "helpful hints" —
things that never seem to appear in the instruction manuals.

In this corner of your newsletter we plan to bring together some of
the talking points which have arisen between members at Branch
meetings. Can <u>you</u> help?

EUROTYPE - does anyone have any experience of this software
package? One of our members would like to know about it.

TELEWRITE - has anybody used this WP package, and if so have they
worked out how to indent the first line of a paragraph?

If you know the answer to any of these queries, please contact the
Newsletter Editor.

(*leave 3 clear line spaces*)

<u>Forthcoming Events - Newtown Branch</u>

15 February   Film Review

 7 March   Links between Education and Industry

11 April   Local Area Networks

 2 May   Annual General Meeting

Visitors are always welcome to attend Branch meetings, so do pass
on news of activities to friends and colleagues.

Recall the document that you keyed in for Task 1 and carry out the revisions indicated below.

File your revised document for printing out later.

TASK ~~1~~ 2   (Candidate's Name)

¶ ~~DRAFT~~   ← (*leave 1 clear line space here*)

TEXTWELL USERS' NEWSLETTER – JANUARY EDITION

Word Processing Problem Corner

One of the benefits of membership of the Textwell Users'
Association is the opportunity to draw on the experience of fellow
members, and to share our own knowledge and "helpful hints" ——   ¶
~~things that never seem to appear in the instruction manuals.~~
                                              from time to time
In this corner of your newsletter/we plan to bring together some of   ʌ
the talking points which have arisen between members at Branch
meetings. Can <u>you</u> help?

EUROTYPE – does anyone have any experience of this software
package? One of our members would like to know about it.

TELEWRITE – has anybody used this WP package, and if so have they
worked out how to indent the first line of a paragraph?
                                                        or if you have a WP problem yourself,
stet   If you know the answer to ~~either~~ any of these queries,/please contact the
Newsletter Editor.

Forthcoming Events – Newtown Branch

15 February   Film Review

 7 March   Links between Education and Industry

11 April   Local Area Networks

 2 May   Annual General Meeting

Visitors are always welcome to attend Branch meetings, so do pass   ʌ *Association*
on news of/activities to friends and colleagues.

TASK 3

A standard document has been prepared and filed on the storage medium. Recall it, and insert the items listed below in the appropriate places. Please note that the numbers (in brackets) are there to indicate where the insertions are to be made, and should <u>not</u> appear in the finished document.

File your completed document for printing out later.

<u>Note:</u> *Your tutor should give you the filename for this document (see page 67).*

<u>TASK 3</u>   (Candidate's Name)

(1)   1800 hours

(2)   Monday 16 January

(3)   Forthcoming Programme of Events

(4)   Membership

(5)   Newsletter

(6)   Educational visits to local companies

TASK 4

The following document has been prepared and filed on the storage medium. Careful proof-reading is necessary, as several mistakes have been made. Recall the document, and compare it with the perfect copy which is given below. Correct all the errors, and file your revised version for printing out later.

Note: *Your tutor should give you the filename for this document (see page 67).*

<u>TASK 4</u>   (Candidate's Name)

TECHNICAL FACTSHEET

Functions of the XS 85 range from sophisticated networking and telecommunications applications to existing WP and document transfer. Features include the 32-bit architecture already found in the XS 90 and XS 100; a disk storage capacity of over five gigabytes; and support of 32 concurrent users, increasing to up to 48 concurrent users with the addition of the optional cache memory which allows configuration of either a second disk IOP or tape IOP, supporting up to eight disk drives.

The basic XS 85 includes 32-bit CPU with 1MB of main memory, expandable to up to 4MB; the XS operating system; one language (Assembler); a 16-port serial IOP; a 48K archiving workstation and one compiler. A wide variety of disk storage devices are available with packaged systems, starting with 90MB.

As a standalone system, the XS 85 offers remote workstation capabilities, mainframe emulation, and local and/or remote networking. The system also addresses other OA functions, such as WP, document transfer, calendar facilities, graphics and a wide range of DP facilities. The use of all available XS peripherals is possible, such as remote archiving and audio workstations; the Personal Computer; the 6400 graphics workstation; matrix, daisy and band printers; tape and disk drives.

Worked solution

Margin of at least 1" ←→

Name must be included here ↑

(Candidate's Name)

<u>TASK 1</u>

CLOSED CAPS + u/s

<u>DRAFT</u>

← *leave 2 clear line spaces*

dash (space either side) ↑

CLOSED CAPS

TEXTWELL USERS' NEWSLETTER – JANUARY EDITION

← *2 clear line spaces (turn up 3)*

Initial caps + u/s → <u>Word Processing Problem Corner</u>

One of the benefits of membership of the Textwell Users'
Association is the opportunity to draw on the experience of
fellow members, and to share our own knowledge and "helpful
dash <u>hints"</u> – things that never seem to appear in the
instruction manuals.

In this corner of your newsletter we plan to bring together
some of the talking points which have arisen between
members at Branch meetings. Can <u>you</u> help?

underscore within body of text ←

dash (space either side)

CLOSED CAPS for paragraph headings → EUROTYPE – does anyone have any experience of this software
package? One of our members would like to know about it.

TELEWRITE – has anybody used this WP package, and if so
have they worked out how to indent the first line of a
paragraph?

If you know the answer to any of these queries, please
contact the Newsletter Editor.

3 clear line spaces (turn up 4) →

<u>Forthcoming Events – Newtown Branch</u> → *Initial caps and underscore*

alignment of dates

15 February	Film Review
7 March	Links between Education and Industry
11 April	Local Area Networks
2 May	Annual General Meeting

→ *Initial caps for Titles of Events*

consistent space between columns

Visitors are always welcome to attend Branch meetings, so
do pass on news of activities to friends and colleagues.

Worked solution

OVERTYPE

DELETE
WORD
&
LINE
SPACES

BLOCK
MARK
AND
MOVE
TO
NEW
POSITION

TASK 2   (Candidate's Name)

TEXTWELL USERS' NEWSLETTER - JANUARY EDITION

Forthcoming Events - Newtown Branch

15 February   Film Review

7 March   Links between Education and Industry

11 April   Local Area Networks

2 May   Annual General Meeting

Visitors are always welcome to attend Branch meetings, so
do pass on news of Association activities to friends and
colleagues.

*use INSERT facility remembering to retain
capital A of Association*

Word Processing Problem Corner

One of the benefits of membership of the Textwell Users'
Association is the opportunity to draw on the experience of
fellow members, and to share our own knowledge and "helpful
hints". ← *use DELETE facility remembering to retain full-stop*

In this corner of your newsletter from time to time we plan   *INSERT facility*
to bring together some of the talking points which have
arisen between members at Branch meetings. Can you help?

EUROTYPE - does anyone have any experience of this software
package? One of our members would like to know about it.

TELEWRITE - has anybody used this WP package, and if so
have they worked out how to indent the first line of a
paragraph?

DELETE
AND
REPLACE
WITH
LONGER WORD

If you know the answer to either of these queries, or if   *INSERT*
you have a WP problem yourself, please contact the   *TEXT*
Newsletter Editor.   *capitals for*
                                                              WP - no
                                                              punctuation,
                                                              remember
                                                              final comma
                                                              after 'yourself'

Worked solution

<u>TASK 3</u>   (Candidate's Name)

A meeting of the Committee of the Newtown Branch of the
Textwell Users' Association will be held in the Conference
Room at 1800 hours on Monday 16 January. ← *Retain full stop*
              ↑   ↑
         Insert (1)   *Insert (2)*
A G E N D A

1   Apologies for absence

2   Minutes of last meeting

3   Matters arising from the minutes

4   Chairman's Report

5   Secretary's Report

6   Treasurer's Report

7   Forthcoming Programme of Events   *Insert (3)*

8   Membership   "   (4)

9   Newsletter   "   (5)

10   Educational visits to local companies   "   (6)

11   Any other business   } *Last two items*
                                   } *on an Agenda*
12   Date of next meeting

Mary Rogers
Branch Secretary

**Worked solution
(the errors have
been highlighted)**

TASK 4 (Candidate's Name)

TECHNICAL FACTSHEET ← (CENTRE)

letter omitted   *insert space*   *letter omitted*
Functions of the (XS85) range from sophisticated networking
and teleco*mm*unications applications to existing WP and
document transfer.   Features include the 32-bit   *insert space*
architecture already found i*n t*he XS 90 and XS 100; a   *repetition of word*
disk storage capacity of (of) over five gigabytes; and
insert space support of 32 concurrent users, increasing to up to 48   *spelling error*
concurrent users with the additio*n* of the optional ca(she)
memory which allows configuration of either a se*co*nd   *transpose letters*
disk IOP or tape ˄ IOP, supporting up to eight disk
(de)rives.   *delete extra space*
   delete extra letter

   spelling error
The basic XS 85 includes 32-bit CPU and 1MB of main
memory, expandable to up to 4MB; the (ZS) o*pe*rating   *transpose letters*
system; one language (Assembler); a 16-port serial IOP;
a 48K archiving workstation and one compiler.   A wide
variety of disk storage devices are available with
pack(e)aged systems, starting with (OONB).   *Spelling error*
   delete extra letter

letter omitted As a standalone system, the XS 85 offers remote   *transpose letters*
workstation capabi(l)ties, mainf(a)rme emulation and local
and/or remote networking.   The system also addresses
delete extra letter other OA functions, such as WP, docu(m)ent transfer,   *Spelling error*
calendar facilit(i)ies, graphics and a wide range of DP   *Spelling error*
facilities.   The use of all available XS peri(pe)rals is
possible, such as remote, archiving and audio
workstations; the Personal Computer; the 6400 graphics
workstation, matrix, daisy and band printers; tape and
disk drives.   *delete comma*

**The 20 errors have been identified.   They may fall into
the following categories:**

omission
spelling
transposition
repetition
punctuation
incorrect spacing or display
text blocked to margin instead of centred
faulty keying in
grammatical agreement

The errors should be corrected on screen using:

centre facility
delete facility
insert facility
overtype facility

Proof-read the final version carefully.

Further practice   The following questions are extracted from recent Elementary Examination Papers which will provide you with the necessary additional practice for the examination.

Again, it will be necessary for the *Specialist Teacher* to create the following two documents on the storage medium prior to your tackling the candidate's paper.

_____

Specialist teacher to store on disk.

TASK 3   (Candidate's Name)

Our Ref (1)

(2)

(3)

Dear (4)

Thank you for your letter of (5) enquiring about membership of the National Trust.

We have great pleasure in enclosing details of membership and if you send us a cheque or postal order for (6) we will be pleased to let you have your membership card and other literature.

As a member you will be entitled to reduced admission at all our properties and gardens and we hope you will spend many happy hours in this way.

Yours sincerely

J NYMANS
Secretary

Enc

TASK 4   (Candidate's Name)

THE NATIONAL TRUST

The National Trust is now almost a century old. It was born on 16 July
1894, in Grosvenor House, Park Lane -kindly made availlable by the Duke of
Westminster of the day. It recieved its formal bapttism six months later
when it was registered under the Companies Act, on 12 January 1895, as "The
national Trust for Places of Historic Interest or natural Beauty". Though
never in any any real sense a sickly child, it proved a slow developer;
indeed, only after its fiftieth birth-day was it to get fully into its
stride. Perhaps it has not reached its oltimate maturity; it is certainly
stil growing, faster than ever. But that is just as well. It will need
all its strength, and more, if it is to meet the challenge of the years to
come.

The Trust's work will never finish. As mechanisation, industrialisation and
population continue to increase, it's responsibility to future generations
becomes every clearer. So does our own to back it to the hilt, secure in
the knowledge that it will Continue as it has for almost a hundred years to
protect and preserve what ever is loveliest in the kingdom, to mainntain and
cherish it, and - above all - to care.

SPECIALIST TEACHER PLEASE NOTE

The above is a proof-reading task. To aid your preparation the
"deliberate mistakes" are circled and care should be taken to ensure that
errors are repeated when this document is created.

TASK 1

You are asked to key-in the following document, following the Invigilator's instructions regarding format and margin settings.

Please copy exactly the layout, line spacing, use of upper and lower case characters, spacing and punctuation. It is not essential that line endings should be identical.

File your completed document for printing out later.

TASK 1   (Candidate's Name)

SHEFFIELD PARK

Sheffield Park is midway between East Grinstead and Lewes in Sussex. The splendour of the gardens is due to the combination of Capability Brown's design of 1775 - trees, sward and serpentine waters - with the inspired planting of the late A G Soames who acquired Sheffield Park in 1909.

For over a quarter of a century he devoted himself to the introduction of all manner of exotic trees and shrubs. Rarely have the conceptions of the 18th and 20th centuries been more happily married.

Autumn, and especially the second half of October, is the great moment for Sheffield Park. Hundreds of trees and shrubs planted especially for their autumn colour create an effect unrivalled in these islands.

Lakes spanned by ornamental bridges, waterfalls and watery vistas recall the spirit of the original layout (though certain of these features are in fact later) while by contrast the cunning planting of the shores speaks volumes about the expertise of the 20th-Century gardener. There are views across the grasses, and white-stemmed birches, all of which contrast with the autumn colours.

These include:

tupelo trees   azaleas
mespiluses   maples
eucryphias   birches
swamp cypresses   larches

Call up a copy of the document about Sheffield Park which you keyed in previously, and carry out the revisions indicated.

Remember that you will need to keep the original version for printing out later, as well as the revised one.

If you notice any keyboarding errors made in Task 1 and carried over, please correct them.

TASK ~~1~~ 2   (Candidate's Name)

SHEFFIELD PARK

u/s Sheffield Park is midway between East Grinstead and Lewes in Sussex. [The   NP
splendour of the gardens is due to the combination of Capability Brown's
design of 1775 - trees, sward and serpentine waters - with the inspired
planting of the late A G Soames who acquired Sheffield Park in 1909. Run on

For over a quarter of a century he devoted himself to the introduction of
all manner of exotic trees and shrubs. Rarely have the conceptions of the
18th and 20th centuries been more happily married.

Autumn, and especially the second half of October, is the great moment for
Sheffield Park. Hundreds of trees and shrubs planted especially for their
autumn colour create an effect unrivalled in these islands.

Lakes spanned by ornamental bridges, waterfalls and watery vistas recall the
ꟼ   spirit of the original layout ~~(though certain of these features are in fact~~
~~later)~~ while by contrast the cunning planting of the shores speaks volumes
lc about the expertise of the 20th-Century gardener. There are views across
the grasses, and white-stemmed birches, all of which contrast with the
autumn colours.

These include:

tupelo trees	azaleas
mespiluses	maples
eucryphias	birches
swamp cypresses	larches

water owing much to the introduction of dark conifers, pampas

TASK 3

A standard document has been prepared and filed on the storage medium. Recall it, and insert the items listed below in the appropriate places. Please note that the numbers are there to indicate where the insertions are to be made, and should not appear in the finished document.

Please date the letter with the date of the examination - do not actually key-in the words "Today's date".

File your completed document for printing out later.

TASK 3   (Candidate's Name)

(1)   JN/ME

(2)   Today's date

(3)   Mrs J Heaton
         18 Penrith Road
         BLACKPOOL
         FY1 6ZR

(4)   Mrs Heaton

(5)   last week

(6)   £15

The following article has been prepared and filed on the storage medium.
Careful proof-reading is necessary, as several mistakes have been made.
Recall the document, and check it against the perfect copy which appears
below. Correct all errors, and file your revised version of the document
for printing out later.

TASK 4   (Candidate's Name)

THE NATIONAL TRUST

The National Trust is now almost a century old. It was born on 16 July
1894, in Grosvenor House, Park Lane - kindly made available by the Duke of
Westminster of the day. It received its formal baptism six months later
when it was registered under the Companies Act, on 12 January 1895, as "The
National Trust for Places of Historic Interest or Natural Beauty". Though
never in any real sense a sickly child, it proved a slow developer; indeed,
only after its fiftieth birthday was it to get fully into its stride.
Perhaps it has not reached its ultimate maturity; it is certainly still
growing, faster than ever. But that is just as well. It will need all its
strength, and more, if it is to meet the challenge of the years to come.

The Trust's work will never finish. As mechanization, industrialization and
population continue to increase, its responsibility to future generations
becomes ever clearer. So does our own; to back it to the hilt, secure in
the knowledge that it will continue as it has for almost a hundred years to
protect and preserve whatever is loveliest in the kingdom, to maintain and
cherish it, and - above all - to care.

Part 2 **Intermediate**

Instructions for Part 2

If you have already acquired basic word processing skills, either by completing the first part of this guide, or through practical experience in the workplace, then you will find the following break-down of the competences required to be successful in the **Intermediate Word Processing** examination appropriate to your needs.

The same approach as in Part 1 has been adopted whereby the skill is firstly *identified*, then *practised* using example material and material from a past PEI examination paper, and then *assessed*. The areas of knowledge and skills to be achieved follow the sequence set out in the **checklist. Competences already covered in the Elementary section** are indicated on the checklist.

You are advised to maintain a **portfolio** of your work with a copy of the **checklist** for recording your progress.

Syllabus

(Time allowed – 1 hour 30 minutes excluding printing time, plus 10 minutes for reading.)

Aim

The aim of the examination is to test the candidate's ability to use a word processor to prepare, process and present realistic business documents with the speed and accuracy which satisfy the assessment criteria.

Target population

The examination is for the person aiming for employment as a word processor operator, capable of working with limited supervision. Such a person should have a good command of English language, and a sound knowledge of office systems and the conventions for display of business documents.

Objectives

The candidate should be able to:

1 Prepare system and disks for use

switch on/log on to the hardware, load the program, handle software media with due regard for security and close down the system

format blank disks and backup work disks

plan and organise work in order to complete the 4 tasks within the time constraints of the examination

2 Create documentation

create new documents

type and display, according to instructions, a variety of business documents from handwritten or typewritten drafts. These could include:

– a business letter
– a memorandum
– a document produced from standard paragraphs
– an article
– a report

and will include documents of more than one page

3 Edit documents

edit documents by responding to written instructions and printers' correction signs

retrieve previously stored documents and amend according to instructions

use underscore, emboldening and centring facilities

change case

insert a character, a word, a phrase, a sentence, a paragraph and line space(s)

insert, at the correct points, items of given information

delete a character, a word, a phrase, a sentence, a paragraph and line space(s)

replace text: a short phrase with a longer phrase, a long phrase with a shorter phrase, and phrases of the same length

use search and replace

move text between pages

4 Set/amend layout

use the tabulation facility to produce tables, indented text and leave space of a specified size

use single or double line spacing as instructed

use ragged or justified right margin as instructed

indent text from both margins

repaginate document appropriately

5 Assemble and/or complete standard documents

assemble documents from standard paragraphs

6 Proof-read and correct documents

identify and correct 'deliberate' mistakes of grammar, spelling, punctuation and typewriting within one task without reference to a correct copy

expand abbreviations – retaining those in common use

proof-read and correct on screen as necessary

7 Save work

save all work correctly on the storage medium

8 Print documents

print documents on either single sheet or continuous stationery in an acceptable format

The examination

The examination will consist of 4 in-tray assignments and the candidate will be assumed to be working in one organisation. Each examination will contain both (a) text to be created and stored, and (b) text to be retrieved for revision. The candidate will be judged on the quality of the printed output he or she produces. The printing of documents during the examination may be carried out at the discretion of the candidates and the Centre.

Assessment

Candidates' performance will be assessed on the criteria of accuracy, presentation and production rate.

To achieve a **Pass** grade, candidates must complete all tasks and must attain a 98.5% standard of accuracy with no more than 8 presentation errors.

A **First Class Pass** will be awarded if candidates achieve a 99% standard of accuracy with no more than 4 presentation errors.

Administration

Prior to the examination, the Specialist Teacher will be expected to prepare and store documents or part documents to be recalled by the candidates during the examination. The Specialist Teacher will also be responsible for assigning names to each candidate's documents and notes about this will accompany the set of papers. At the end of the printing the Specialist Teacher must erase all files from the storage media.

Checklist – Intermediate

		Aided	Date	Unaided	Date
17	**Organising work tasks** Organise work tasks by extracting work details from job sheets selecting appropriate stationery.				
18 **18.1** **18.2**	**Changing margins and line spacing from the default settings** Set margins other than the default to adjust the line length. Use single or double line spacing.				
19	**Using display features** Use the system's display features to underline, centre, embolden text and change case.				

20.1
 	
20.2
	Using the tab key to set indented paragraphs and display in columns
	Set tabs to: indent text
	          align text in numbered items using para tab
	          display material in columns
	          leave space of specified size
	
	Keying in text and figures from amended manuscript				

21.1 **21.2**	**Presenting documents in an acceptable style** Present in correct and acceptable form and to mailable standard, a variety of business documents, including multi-page documents, eg: • business letter • memorandum • document produced from standard paragraphs • article • report **Amending text and design** Insert, delete and replace text. Expand abbreviations – retaining those in common use. Proof-read on screen a document containing obvious errors of keying in, agreement, punctuation and spelling within one task, without reference to a correct copy.				
22	**Justification** Use the right-hand margin justification feature to present documents to an acceptable standard.				

23	**The search and replace facilities** Edit or revise a document file by using the search and replace facility to locate a specified string and replace as instructed.			
24	**Moving text within and between pages and repaginating** Edit or revise a document file by using the move facility to move text between pages. Repaginate a document.			
25	**Standard paragraphs** Assemble a document from previously stored paragraphs and insert variable information at in-fill points as required.			
26.1	**Intermediate examination questions** Ensure that all competences learned in Part 2 meet the required standard for the Intermediate examination. In addition the following skills should be achieved and demonstrated throughout Part 2 of this guide.			
26.2	**Ensure consistency throughout a task in the style and form of presentation** • abbreviations • words/figures • words/symbols (dash/hyphen) • punctuation (open or closed) • paragraphing (including number or letter paragraphs) • line spacing between paragraphs and after headings			
26.3	**Proof-read on screen a document containing obvious errors of keying-in, agreement, punctuation and spelling within one task, without reference to a correct copy**			
26.4	**Plan and organise work within a time constraint**			

Organise work tasks by extracting work details from job sheets, selecting appropriate stationery

In the PEI Intermediate Word Processing Examination you will be expected to respond to instructions which mirror the way work is organised in the 'real' office situation. The 4 tasks which you are required to carry out take the form of **in-tray** exercises and you will have been given a brief scenario describing your **work situation**.

An *example* word processing request form is illustrated below.

Example

WORD PROCESSING REQUEST FORM

Task number: ...4...... Author's name:...M. Garner......

Create a document: ..... New document name: ....

Edit a document: ..✓... Existing document name: ....MG4......
Rename document as: ....

Standard paragraphs are stored as:

....

....

....

Type of copy: Draft: .... Final: ...✓.........

Line spacing: 1 .... 2 .... As copy: ...✓.........

No of copies required: ......1........................
Paper size: A4 .✓... A5 ..... Portrait: .✓... Landscape: .....

Date required: ..Today.... Retain on file: .✓. Delete: ....

SPECIAL INSTRUCTIONS:

Our Junior typed the attached ^report and hasn't corrected the errors. Please will you correct it and print me a copy with my additional amendments. Justified right margin, please. Put GGC as Greensdale Garden Centre with initial caps, please.

Test your competence

Answer the following questions based on the *example* Word Processing Request Form to make sure you have understood the instructions given.

1   Who is the author of the document?

2   Are you creating a new document or editing an existing document?

3   Is this document going to be revised at a later stage?

4   If the answer is yes, how do you know this?

5   Is the author a good speller? If not, why not?

6   Will you need to alter the default margins?

7   What line spacing is required?

8   How many copies of the document are required?

9   What type of business document will you be preparing?

10   What type of right margin is required?

11   Will it be necessary to store the document on disk?

Practice from the paper

Study the attached Word Processing Request Form and answer the following questions to test your understanding of the instructions:

1   Which department are you working for?

2   What are your employer's initials?

3   Is the document already stored on disk?

4   What special instruction is there with regard to printing the document?

5   Does the document require editing?

6   What line-spacing is required?

7 How urgent is the task?

8 Would it be acceptable to print out on a piece of A4 with the longer edge to the top?

9 Under what file name is the document stored?

10 Will the document require further editing?

WORD PROCESSING REQUEST FORM

Task number: ..3...... Author's name:..T.K. Johnson. (Personnel)

Create a document: ..... New document name: ....

Edit a document: ...✓.... Existing document name: ..PER 4.......
Rename document as: ....

Standard paragraphs are stored as:

....

....

....

Type of copy: Draft: .... Final: ...✓.............

Line spacing: 1 .... 2 ...✓...... As copy: ....

No of copies required: ..I.................................
Paper size: A4 .✓... A5 ..... Portrait: ..✓.. Landscape: .....

Date required: ..Today... Retain on file: ..✓. Delete: ....

SPECIAL INSTRUCTIONS:

Amend, proof-read and correct this document –
don't forget to change the line spacing.
Ragged right-hand margin, please.

18 Changing margins and line spacing from the default settings

Set margins other than the default to adjust the line length. Alter the line spacing to other than the default of single line spacing

At the Intermediate level you will be asked to adjust the margins of part of a document to indent text from both margins.

You will also be asked to leave space of a specified size.

Most word processing systems have a **status line** which is either located at the top or the bottom of the screen. This provides the operator with information about the page layout. On some systems a **ruler line** is also displayed which shows the location of the left and right margin and the position of the tab stops. You will need to ensure that you follow the screen carefully.

Note: Make sure that you do not leave less than the space requested. You will also be asked to use single and double line spacing. The number of clear lines left between lines of text can usually be altered by giving a single command. The new line spacing is generally displayed on the **status line**.

Example

```
L       Tab                                                          R
─────────────────────────────────────────────────────────────────
12      18                                                          84
```

PRESS
TAB
KEY TO
TAKE
CURSOR
TO
INDENT
POINT

→   Since its introduction in July 1983, Cardcash has gone from strength to strength, with each year seeing new features and services added.

For instance Cardcash machines are now connected to the LINK network. This means access to an additional 1,500 LINK machines.

```
    L       Tab                               R
    ─────────────────────────────────────────
    24      29                                72
```

We are happy to recommend Safety First, the card protection scheme which, for just a few pounds a year, provides you with valuable protection against the loss or theft of all your plastic cards.

For those of you holidaying abroad this year, don't forget your local branch provides a full travellers cheques and foreign currency service.

Create a new file using a suitable file name and key in the following, altering the margin settings as you go on.

Save the file to disk and print out one copy.

The Hong Kong Telephone Company is pleased to announce the launch of its improved customer service so that when new developments occur and new services become available these will be instantly relayed to you.

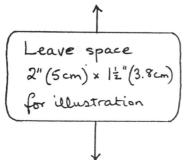

Leave space
2" (5cm) × 1½" (3.8cm)
for illustration

You will see from the illustrated 'cordless' phone that the Hong Kong Telephone Company can help you reach that friend or client wherever you are.

Remember the model also includes a feature for those frequently dialled numbers that you so often forget!

Why don't you send for our new, free, 52-page catalogue? This contains our complete range of phones including the smart and sophisticated telephone and answering machine illustrated here.

We can also advise you on how to get your messages when you are on the move.

If you are interested, please return the reply form below and you will receive your free copy without delay.

Further practice

Please create a new document. Key in the following, altering the line lengths as indicated.

COLLEGE BOOKSHOP ← (Spaced caps plse.)

uc You are invited to support and use a college bookshop run
uc by Avon Books as part of the college library service.

Its aims are to:

Inset by 1" (2.5cm) from both margins

* Provide an effective order and supply service to all
  students (full and part-time).
* Stock books recommended for essential reading and
  assignment work.
* Eliminate the frustration currently experienced by
  students and staff when trying to obtain new or
  popular titles.

The bookshop will operate as follows:

From now until the end of term, Avon Books will take
orders from lecturers for books required by staff and
students next academic year.

Insert line space

Commencing September, a supply of the recommended titles
will be available for sale from the bookshop, which will
be set up by the refectory. on the ground floor near reception
The shop will be open for a period of three weeks at the
following times:

#/ 10.30 am – 2.00pm   Monday – Friday
#/   5.30 pm – 7.15pm   Selected evenings (exact days to be
                                                arranged)

Inset by 1" (2.5cm) from both margins

Throughout the rest of the year, books may be ordered at
u.c. any time on a mail order basis via the college library.
uc   The bookshop organiser will visit the college once a week
     to pick up and deliver orders and ensure the smooth
     running of the service.

N.B. All books are supplied on a sale or return basis.
     Orders can be made for course and non-course items,
     both in bulk and individually.
run on   A 10% discount is offered on all departmental
         orders. Teleordering ensures a fast and efficient
         service.

double line spacing

Check your success

Did you set out the heading in *spaced capitals?* ☐

Did you respond to the instruction to change the capitalisation of College and College Library Service? ☐

Did you alter the line length as instructed in order to inset the text by 1" (2.5 cm)? ☐

Did you insert the line spaces and spaces in the times before pm? ☐

Did you run on? ☐

Did you key in the last paragraph in double-line spacing? ☐

Did you proof-read carefully for accuracy? ☐

19   Using display features

Use the system's display features to underline, centre, embolden text and change case

Your system will have certain automatic features which help the operator to present work attractively. The **underline** and **centring** features have already been covered in the Elementary section of the guide (*see* checklist references 5 and 6).

Emboldening text is achieved by the *printer* going over the text more than once to achieve a darker type. This is a particularly useful feature for **emphasising** text.

The operator should position the cursor on the screen at the beginning of the text to be emboldened and key in the appropriate command to embolden the specific amount of text. The text is then typed and it is usually necessary to 'turn off' the emboldening command. The emboldening of the text occurs at **printout**.

You will often be asked to change the case – from lower case to upper case (eg small letters to capitals) or vice versa.

Example

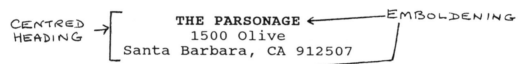

CENTRED HEADING →

THE PARSONAGE ← EMBOLDENING
1500 Olive
Santa Barbara, CA 912507

SANTA BARBARA. THE PARSONAGE. Lovely spacious rooms with private baths. Light and airy rooms. Unique three-room honeymoon suite with ocean, city and mountain view. Close to everything. Of interest nearby is the Santa Barbara Mission, theatres, restaurants and shops.

RATES AND RESTRICTIONS: $65 to $105. Full breakfast.
<u>No children under 14</u>. **No pets.**

Continuous underscore

＊＊＊＊＊

Open a new document file and display the following effectively.
Save to disk and print out one copy.

FAIRWAYS COUNTRY INN ← *Centre & bold*

OSTERVILLE ← *u/s & bold*

Antique filled rooms and common rooms.
Private baths. Located on 7th fairway of
Wianno Country Club.
Short walk to quaint village.

1 mile to beach.

Of interest nearby National Seashore,
Crosby Yacht Basin, Sandwich glass *uc*
uc museum, Heritage Plantation.

bold RATES : double from $55 high season
$40 Spring/Fall. $30 off-season.

Extra person $10 per night

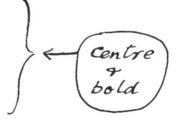

105 Parkes Road
OSTERVILLE
MA 02653

Tel: 514-326-2493   ← *Centre & bold*

**Practice from the
paper**

The following task extracted from a past paper tests the following competences:

Checklist reference 17   extracting work details from job sheet
Checklist reference 18.1 setting margins other than the default
Checklist reference 18.2 altering the line spacing
Checklist reference 19   using display features, including emboldening
Checklist reference 20.1 displaying material in columns (*see* Elementary 3)

Checklist reference 20.2 keying in text and figures from amended manuscript involving
responding to printers' correction signs (*see* Elementary 4)
Checklist reference 21.1 business document – memorandum
Checklist reference 26.2 consistency of presentation

Note: Before tackling the task, please make sure that you are familiar with those competences covered in the Elementary section.

WORD PROCESSING REQUEST FORM

Task number: 3.	Author's name: Richard Parks
Create a document: ✓	New document name: RP3
Edit a document:	Existing document name: ....
	Rename document as: ....
Standard paragraphs are stored as:	
Type of copy: Draft: .... Final: ..✓.	
Line spacing: 1 .... 2 .... As copy: .✓..	
No of copies required: ..1........	
Paper size: A4 .✓.. A5 .... Portrait: ✓... Landscape: ...	
Date required: ..Today........ Retain on file: .... ✓ Delete:	

SPECIAL INSTRUCTIONS:

Please complete the reference with your initials
in lower case & date today.

MEMORANDUM ← (Spaced caps & centred)

Please embolden the text shown

To: John Carter   REF: RP/

From: Richard Parks   DATE:

DETAILS OF WINNERS FOR ANNUAL PRIZE PRESENTATION
VENUE: BANKFIELD HOTEL, BAKER ROAD, ILKLEY   } centre

stet I have ~~at last~~ *now* received the final results for our Annual Prize Presentation as listed below. You should (have already) trs received, ~~from other members of the cttee,~~ details of the menu for the evening from the hotel & the list of toasts, as agreed at the last meeting.

run on Can you let the printer have all these details as soon as possible so that he can get the cards printed in the usual form.

EVENT	FIRST	SECOND
STONES TROUGH TROPHY	B Brown	J Carter
ECONOMY RUN	N Greenwood	R Calvert
CAPTAIN'S ROSE BOWL	P Smith	L Thomas
FUN-NIGHT	L Thomas	T Hepworth
NAVIGATIONAL SCATTER	P Dunn	K Lees
~~ACASTER MALBIS TRIAL~~	~~R Calvert~~	~~P Peters~~
~~SCAMMONDEN AUTOTEST~~	~~M Mathews~~	~~P Smith~~
~~CROMWELL HILL CLIMB~~	~~N Whittaker~~	~~H Wilde~~
~~A1 PRODUCTION TEST~~	~~S Leonard~~	~~D Parker~~

trs / Double line spacing

Check your success

Did you create a new document file and retain it on file? ☐

Did you centre and use *spaced capitals* for the heading? ☐

Did you complete the reference with your initials? ☐

Did you insert today's date? ☐

Did you *centre* and *embolden* the subject heading? ☐

Did you retain 'at last' in the first sentence? □

Did you transpose 'have' and 'already'? □

Did you *run-on* the second paragraph? □

Did you set up the *tabs* for the 3 column table? □

Did you leave equal space between the columns? □

Did you allow for the longest item in each column? □

Did you follow the instruction for *double line spacing?* □

Did you *transpose* the second and third lines of the table? □

Did you proof-read carefully before printing out? □

Using the tab key to set indented paragraphs

Setting tabs to:

- **indent text**
- **align text in numbered items using para tab**
- **display material in columns** (*see* also 3)
- **leave space of a specified size**

Keying in text and figures from amended manuscript

Clearing existing default tab settings and creating new tab points has already been covered in the Elementary section checklist reference 3.

In order to create **indented** paragraphs, a tab is set 5 spaces in from the left-hand margin, and then the operator presses the **tab** key so that the cursor goes quickly to this point. The remainder of the paragraph is keyed in using the *wraparound* feature *so that* the rest of the text starts at the *left margin.*

When creating paragraphs with numbered points or side headings, it is necessary to create a *temporary* left hand margin at the tab point so that the text *wraps* to this point and *not* to the existing left margin. It is usually necessary first to *set a tab* at the required point and then to carry out an additional command or key sequence so that the text *wraps to the point of the tab.* The special command sequence is usually cancelled when the return key is pressed. This method can be used for leaving a space of a specified size at the left margin.

Examples
Numbered items with para tab feature

Text wrapped to TAB POINT

TAB POINT

1 Keep long hair fixed back when using your printer, don't let long hair get caught in the mechanism – it could be extremely painful. ↵ RETURN BREAKS TEMPORARY MARGIN

2 Keep all liquids away from the keyboard, the disk drives, terminals and printers.

TAB POINT (ALLOWING FOR LONGEST WORD IN SIDE HEADING)

Text wrapped to TAB POINT

Feed Deck	The feed deck will take several letters at the same time and feed them automatically one by one along the envelope path.
Automatic Feed Adjustment	This feature allows any size or shape of envelope to be opened. The cutting knife automatically adjusts itself to thick or thin letters.
Stacker	The opened envelopes are stacked automatically and neatly in the stack, ready for removal and easy extraction of their contents.

Test your competence

Open a new document file and key in the following memo. A left margin of a minimum of 1"/2.5 cm is required. Follow the instructions carefully. Save to disk and print one copy.

MEMORANDUM ← *Bold Centre + spaced caps*

To James Post
From William Metzinger
Subject Production Release 4903-411-002
Date

Indent This production release is for 500 Type
uc 203 motors with a shaft diameter of 8 mm. Since this production run is small, the following tooling should be reviewed:

indent 1 The slot insulating machine will not run the insulation needed for this motor and a new forming roller is needed.

leave a clear line space between paragraphs

2 A saddle to suit a 8 mm diameter shaft was requested for the lathe to turn the commutator.

3 The jaws of the magnetizer require polishing because paint is being damaged during the magnetizing operation.

4 A lock is required on the magnetizer
5 black panel to ~~prevent~~ stop tampering stet with the charging controls.

WORD PROCESSING REQUEST FORM

Task number: .3..   Author's name: J. B. Powell..................

Create a document: ✓....   New document name: ..JBP1..................

Edit a document: ....   Existing document name: ....

Rename document as: ....

Standard paragraphs are stored as: ....

. . . .

Type of copy: Draft: ....   Final: .✓..

Line spacing: 1 ✓..   2 ....   As copy: ....

No of copies required: ..1........

Paper size: A4 .✓..   A5 ....   Portrait: ✓...   Landscape: ...

Date required: ..Today.........   Retain on file: ✓...   Delete: ......

SPECIAL INSTRUCTIONS:

Please type the attached.

Memorandum ← (caps)   (Candidate's Name)

To: Mrs Lane   cc Mrs Sharp
    Mrs Hall   Miss Rushmore

Date: (today)   Ref: JBP/(your initials)
From: Mrs Powell

Subject: Interviews — Mrs Lane's PA

Timetable ← (centre this heading)

Time	Details	Contact
0930-1030	Welcome to the Company: the Company's background and history	Ms Powell
1030-1045	Coffee	
1045-1230	Skills testing: Audio-typing, typing and shorthand	Mrs Sharp
1230-1330	Lunch	Mrs Hall Mrs Lane
1330-1430	Interviews	Ms Powell Mrs Lane Mrs Hall

Check your success

Did you add your initials to the reference? ☐

Did you use today's date? ☐

Did you centre the heading 'Timetable'? ☐

Did you leave equal spaces between the columns in the table? ☐

Did you allow sufficient space for the longest line in each column of the table? ☐

Did you leave space either side of the 'dash' in the times, eg 0930 – 1030? ☐

Did you retain the use of the 24-hour clock? ☐

21 Presenting documents in an acceptable style Amending text and design

Present in correct and acceptable form, and to mailable standard, a variety of business documents, including multi-page documents, eg:

- **business letter**
- **memorandum**
- **document produced from standard paragraphs (*see* Section 25)**
- **article**
- **report**

Insert, delete and replace text

Expand abbreviations – retaining those in common use

Proof-read onscreen a document containing obvious errors of keying in, agreement, punctuation and spelling within one task, without reference to a correct copy

You have already met business letters, memorandums, reports and articles in the course of keying in and editing documents in previous tasks. If you need further assistance on acceptable layout, *see* the Appendix. Producing a document from standard paragraphs is covered in Section 25.

Throughout the paper, you will be asked to insert and delete a character, word, phrase, sentence, paragraph and line space(s). You will also be required to replace a short phrase with a longer phrase, a long phrase with a shorter phrase, and phrases of the same number of words. Whenever you make an amendment, ensure that you leave consistent spacing between words and between paragraphs.

One task will contain 'deliberate' mistakes that have been keyed in by the Specialist Teacher for you to identify and correct. You will not have the corrected copy to check against, so you must be very careful to proof-read the tasks thoroughly and not to overlook any errors. Use your Spellcheck facility to help you with this.

There will be several abbreviations spread throughout the tasks. These will usually be followed by a full stop, eg hv. (have), co. (company), bn. (been), wd. (would), rd. (road) and mag. (magazine). These must be expanded. Where you see the & (ampersand) symbol in the text, this must also be expanded unless it is part of a company name. Some abbreviations should *not* be expanded – 'eg', 'NB', 'ie'.

Example
Copy for amendment

INDUCTION PROGRAMME

Personnel Policy

(remove 1 linespace)

This Policy sets out the blueprint ~~for~~ *of* an Induction Programme for
all staff new to the Clarkton Manufacturing Co Ltd. Although it
is recomended that their should be a common-to - all new staff
aspect, it will be for the individaul delatrments to setermine
fthe extend and and type of the Induction process necessary

The proces can be split into 3 parts:

¶ Instruction training: ~~the basic~~ instruction in the routines and
and procedures which are required to enable the new employee to
performt he duties required

¶ Introduction: what happens when a new employee*s* start*s* on the first day

Orientation: formal ~~organised course~~ *session* introducing the *new* employee to
the wider aspects of the job. *This includes the structure of the company.*

The prog. wl. include such items as:

introduction to colleagues

lunch & coffee breaks

flexable working hrs.

fire regs.

Safety regulations.

Corrected copy

INDUCTION PROGRAMME

Personnel Policy

This Policy sets out the blueprint of an Induction Programme for
all staff new to the Clarkton Manufacturing Co Ltd. Although it
is recommended that there should be a common-to-all new staff
aspect, it will be for the individual departments to determine
the extent and type of the Induction process necessary.

The process can be split into 3 parts:

Instruction training: instruction in the routines and procedures
which are required to enable the new employee to perform the
duties required

Introduction: what happens when new employees start on the first
day

Orientation: formal session introducing the new employee to the
wider aspects of the job. This includes the structure of the
company.

The programme will include such items as:

introduction to colleagues
lunch and coffee breaks
flexible working hours
fire regulations
safety precautions.

On a new document file and key in the following draft. There are mistakes in the typescript that must be corrected, and please expand all abbreviations. Print out one copy.

caps & underline

to yr satisfaction.

Draft for Chairmans Address *by J P Donovan*   (Candidate's Name)

Good evening colleagues and wel come to Dexton Hall. I trsut that you have alll had a good journey, despite the weather and that your accomodation is satisfactory. For those who have brought children with you there is a regular security patrol so that you may enjoy yourselves in the evening.

The purpose of this weekend seminar is to aquaint you with the National and Branch organisation of the Union and how you might make the best use of the Union facilities for yourselves and your members.

You will split into seminar groups, according to to the Branch office that you hold, and the semniar leaders will show you to the rooms concerned at the end of this session. (A)

underline

If there are any problems regarding the course or acommodation, then you should contact Jim poole. he will be in the course teams office in Room G27 and may also be contacted in the bar at lunchtime and evenign.

You have each been supplied with a a course assesment form and I shall obliged if you will complete every section so that we may make full use of your comments when organising further seminars.

(B)

You have a very full programe but that does not mean that their will not be time to enjoy yourselves and I look forward to seeing you at the Semianr Dinner tomrrow night.

Have an anjoyable weekend.

Insert this paragraph at (A) [Periodically during the weekend we wl. reassemble at this location for full discussion sessions on the points covered by your individual groups.

Insert this paragraph at (B) [It is said that you only get as much out of anything as you put into it. This is certainly the case as far as this weekend is concerned. You will learn about existing practices but we are also looking to you for ideas on how we can improve services for members. Do not be afraid to criticise current practices & suggest alternatives.

Test your competence

Open a new document file and key in the following letter. There are mistakes that must be corrected, and please expand all abbreviations. Print out one copy.

Mr J P Donovan
16 Beckett Park
LEEDS
LS14 9PR

Dear John

Here is a copy of the draft report that I propose to present to the Welfare Secretaries' Group at the National Seminar. Will you please read it throught & make any amendments you feel appropriate? Can you return it to me quickly so that I can get it printed & into the delegate folders.

1 FINANCIAL IMPLICATIONS
At the end of the period 1984/85 total Membership was 1,038,000 with each member paying an annual subscription to the Welfare Fund of approximately £1.

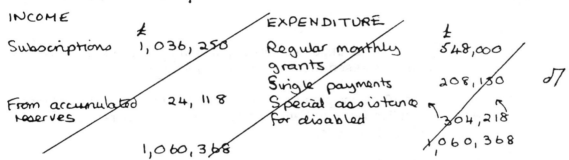

INCOME	£	EXPENDITURE	£
Subscriptions	1,036,250	Regular monthly grants	548,000
		Single payments	208,150
From accumulated reserves	24,118	Special assistance for disabled	304,218
	1,060,368		1,060,368

It can be seen that without the accumulated reserves, wh. at present amount to approx. £3 million, the Welfare Fund wd. be in severe financial difficulties.

2 WELFARE CASES
Previously the majority of Welfare cases were retired members. However, with current trends in employment the majority are now young serving members & those who have recently been made redundant.

NB It is perhaps time for an increase in the proportion of subscriptions for welfare purposes.

Yours sincerely

Jim Barron

The following task is taken from a past PEI Examination paper. Please note that in the examination the *recalled task* will have been set up on the candidate's disk by the *tutor*. The first part of this task may therefore be prepared for you by your tutor or you may key in the document yourself.

Note to the Specialist Teacher

Please key in the following text with a minimum left-hand margin of 1" (2.5 cm) and line-spacing as shown.

TASK 4   (Candidate's Name)

Ref   PH/(your initials)

(Today's date)

The Manager
Airport Hotel
Runway Road
MANCHESTER
M4 6DM

Dear Sir
Last Wednsday, we held an important meeting at your hotel and I am sorry to say that we were not at all pleased with the service we recieved.

a meeting room for 10 person's had been reserved but when my Sales Manager arrived at the Reception Desk at 9 am he was informed that there was norecord of a reservation having been made.

Fortunately. he had with him a letter from you confirming this reservation.

Under the circumstances, I feel that we should be given a reduction in the charge for this room as it was not a normal meeting room and we certainly did not receive the usual standard of service that we expect form your hotel.

I look forward to your comments.

Your faithfully

Marketing Directer

SPECIALIST TEACHER PLEASE NOTE

The above is a proof-reading task. To aid your preparation the "deliberate mistakes" are circled and care should be taken to ensure that errors are repeated when this document is created.

The examination requires you to recall the stored **draft** which will have been keyed in by your **tutor** and follow the instructions given on the *word processing request form*.
    This particular task tests the following competences:

Checklist reference 17   extracting work details from job sheet
Checklist reference 20.2   keying in text from manuscript
Checklist reference 21.2   correcting obvious errors
Checklist reference 21.2   expanding abbreviations
Checklist references 9, 10, 21   using basic editing skills – insert, delete etc
Checklist reference 21.1   business document – letter

WORD PROCESSING REQUEST FORM

Task number: ...4..... Author's name: *L. Warren*..........

Create a document: ..... New document name: ....

Edit a document: .✓..... Existing document name: ....

Rename document as: ....

Standard paragraphs are stored as:

....

....

....

Type of copy: Draft: .... Final: .✓..............

Line spacing: 1 ...✓....... 2 .... As copy: ....

No of copies required: ...*1*.............................

Paper size: A4 ..✓.. A5 ..... Portrait: .✓.. Landscape: .....

Date required: ..*Today*.. Retain on file: ..✓. Delete: ....

SPECIAL INSTRUCTIONS:

TASK 4   (Candidate's Name)

Ref   PH/(your initials)

(Today's date)

The Manager
Airport Hotel
Runway Road
MANCHESTER
M4 6DM

Dear Sir
Last Wednsday, we held an important meeting at your hotel and I am sorry to say
that we were not at all pleased with the service we recieved. *I should be grateful
if you would take note of my comments.*
a meeting room for 10 person's had been reserved but when my Sales Manager
arrived at the Reception Desk at 9 am he was informed that there was norecord of
a reservation having been made.

Fortunately. he had with him a letter from you confirming this/reservation.   *L particular*

Under the circumstances, I feel that we should be given a reduction in the charge
for this room as it was not a normal meeting room and we certainly did not receive
the usual standard of service/that we expect form your hotel.   *L and facilities*

~~I look forward to your comments.~~
~~sincerely~~
Your ~~faithfully~~

H

stet

Marketing Director

*At 9.45 am, 15 minutes before the meeting was due to
start, he was offered a small meeting room. There was
little time to prepare the room and the accomm.
was cramped.*

*Coffee and biscuits had bn. requested for 11am but they
did not arrive &, although our Sales Manager was
assured that a table for 10 would be available in the
restaurant at 1pm, the delegates had to sit at two
separate tables.*

110 Word Processing

Practice from the paper

The following task is taken from a past PEI Examination paper.
This particular task tests the following competences:

Checklist reference 17	extracting work details from job sheet
Checklist reference 18	altering margins
Checklist reference 20.2	keying in text from manuscript
Checklist reference 22	using right margin justification
Checklist reference 19	using the underline and centre facilities
Checklist references 9, 10, 21	using basic editing skills – insert, delete, etc
Checklist reference 21.2	expanding abbreviations
Checklist reference 21.1	business document – report

Task number: ..*3*....... Author's name: .*L.Warren*..............

Create a document: .*✓*.... New document name: ....

Edit a document: .... Existing document name: ....

Rename document as: ....

Standard paragraphs are stored as:

....

....

....

Type of copy: Draft: .... Final: ..*✓*..............

Line spacing: 1 ..*✓*........ 2 .... As copy: ....

No of copies required: .*1*..............................

Paper size: A4 .*✓*... A5 ..... Portrait: .*✓*... Landscape: .....

Date required: ..*Today*... Retain on file: *✓*... Delete: ....

SPECIAL INSTRUCTIONS:

TASK 3   (Candidate's Name)

THE PHARMADRUG COMPANY ⎫
REGISTRATION   REVIEW ⎬ centre and underscore.

PRODUCT	LICENCE NO	STATUS
MAXCHEW	PL8423	Submitted April last yr., awaiting approval from the commission
DITREX	PL8425	Approved last month
ALSIP	PL8501	A variation has bn. submitted and we are awaiting approval
FLUSTROL	PL8504	Failed submission due to insufficient data Resubmit in March. Info. is awaited from Drs Brown and Logan
COFSIP	PL8566	Failed submission. No plans to resubmit until new data is available

(Leave 4 clear lines)

indent 1" (2.5cm) from both margins →

The mean time to approval for abridged submissions can be misleading as some simple submissions can be dealt with quickly. Complex submissions (eg new indication) need extensive evaluation by the pharmacy or medical sections, or both. These usually take the longest time.

Check your success   Did you centre and underscore both lines of the heading?   ☐

Did you underline the column headings?   ☐

Did you leave 4 clear line spaces after the columns?   ☐

Did you indent the last paragraph 1" (2.5 cm) from *both* margins?   ☐

Did you expand yr., bn., Info., Drs.?   ☐

22 Justification

Use the right hand margin justification feature to present documents to an acceptable standard

A right-hand margin which is completely straight is said to be **justified**. When work is keyed in on a word processor it is possible to give an instruction so that at **printout** the text has a straight right margin. The system achieves this by inserting spaces between words and letters.

Example

A Typical Tudor Banquet

On arrival, guests assemble in the ancient Suttons Room with its pleasant bar.

At 8 pm the Court Chamberlain greets the assembled guests and outlines the evening's entertainment, at the same time introducing the Lord and Lady of the Revels, serving wenches and entertainers.

Test your competence

Open a new document file and key in the following. Print out with **right justification**.

THE BAY TREE ← _centre_

single spacing please

Introduction

This Building was formerly the George Inn. Much of the

original building, dating back to 1314 is preserved in the

NP   Restaurant. [The carved heads on the beams in the Old George

Room are of Edward II/and his Queen Isabella. William   ∠ _(1307-1327)_

Shakespeare and his players are believed to have played

in the Courtyard and Oliver Cromwell slept here on his way

to join the army/. The Inn is also mentioned by Charles   ∠ _in 1645_

Dickens in "Little Dorrit".

Martin Chuzzlewit

The Main Staircase

This is a rare example of an early 18th century staircase, of

uc fine workmanship. _s_ome of the balusters show signs of charred

wood. This was caused by a fire in the Old George Hotel in

1947.

SUTTONS ROOM

The Tudor Mantel *piece*   ⌃

piece

This handsome mantel⌃ contains 4 meda⌿llion portraits of a   ⌃ ᛞ

merchant his wife, son and ͩaughter-in-law. The me͵n are   ⌃

wearing biretta hats and all 4 have ruffs. *By the dress, the*

portraits can be dated at about 1485.

The Exposed Writing

n

On an exposed bea⌿, facing the window, is written: ᛞ

"Have God before thine eyes, who searcheth hart and raines,
and live according to his lawe, then glory is they gaines".

THE OLD GEORGE ROOM

The Heads of Edward II and Queen Isabella

These heads on the beam-ends in the far part of the room date

from about 1314. ~~Queen Isabella was a somewhat fiery lady who~~   ᛞ

~~diapproved of her husband's friends. She had him done to~~

~~death in Berkeley Castle.~~

(*The word "raines" means "lives".*)

Practice from the paper

The following task extracted from a past paper tests these competences:

Checklist reference 17   extracting work details from a job sheet
Checklist reference 18   altering margins other than the default
Checklist reference 20.1 using tabs
Checklist reference 20.2 keying in text from a manuscript
Checklist reference 21.1 a business letter
Checklist reference 26.2 consistency in style of presentation

WORD PROCESSING REQUEST FORM

Task number: 2.	Author's name: ...D. Ludberry...............
Create a document: ✓..	New document name: ....
Edit a document:	Existing document name: ....
	Rename document as: ....
Standard paragraphs are stored as:	
Type of copy: Draft: ✓.. Final:	
Line spacing: 1 ..✓ 2 .... As copy:	
No of copies required: ...1........	
Paper size: A4 ✓.. A5 .... Portrait: ✓.. Landscape: ...	
Date required: ...today....... Retain on file: ✓.. Delete:	

SPECIAL INSTRUCTIONS:

Please key-in & print a draft copy of the following circular letter with a justified right-hand margin.

Leave a minimum 1" (2.5cm) left margin. Add your own initials to the Ref. Do not leave extra spaces for a name & address.

Ref DL/
Date as Postmark

Dear

We are now making our plans for a conference for the firm's major retail outlets. The objective is to give up-to-date information on our products and policy and to provide some good advice through lectures by experts and discussions with colleagues.

Inset at least 1/2 inch (1.3 cm)

PROGRAMME OF EVENTS
Queens Hotel, London SW1 3HL
Thursday 18 September – Saturday 20 September

Thursday		Friday		Saturday
Reception	7pm	Lecture 9.30 am		Return home
Dinner	8 pm	Dinner Party 8.30 pm		
Lecture	10 pm			

After dinner on Thursday a lecture will be given by the head of our Research and Development Section and he will be explaining in detail some new features which will soon be standard on our products.

On Friday morning there will be an illustrated lecture of sales techniques given by the new manager of the Sales Board. The afternoon and the next morning will be spent in discussion among ourselves, and if there is a particular topic that you would like included please inform me at an early date.

u.c. The Dinner Party on Friday evening will be given by the _directors_ with the Chairman as our principal speaker. An invitation is extended to your wife to accompany you and I look forward

NP to seeing you both. [I am sure we shall enjoy this conference and find it very useful.

type at left margin → Yours sincerely   (4 clear spaces)
David Ludberry
Sales Manager

Check your success

Did you use A4 portrait paper? ☐

Did you add your initials to the reference? ☐

Did you leave a minimum left-hand margin of 1"/2.5 cm? ☐

Did you type 'Date as Postmark?' ☐

Did you leave extra space for the addressee? ☐

Did you *inset* by at least ½" (1.3 cm) the programme of events? ☐

Did you leave 4 clear spaces after the complimentary close? ☐

Did you use an initial capital for the word 'Directors' in the final paragraph? ☐

Did you proof-read carefully? ☐

23 The search and replace facilities

Edit or revise a document file by using the search and replace facility to locate a specified string and replace as instructed

The search and replace facility is a useful one which allows you quickly to locate a string of characters (a group of figures, letters or symbols). When requested to locate a particular string the cursor goes directly to the first occurrence of that string. You can then carry out the replacement either **manually** or **automatically** depending on the command you give. The advantage of using automatic replacement is the speed with which the system locates every occurrence of the string and replaces it.

However, the system may locate occurrences of the string which you had not wanted to replace, eg the word *the* when it occurs within another word (*then*). It is possible to give further commands to ensure that the system only looks for *whole* words or to ensure that it only finds a particular string if it begins with a capital letter. It is often safer to carry out the replacement manually, although this will depend on the length of the document file.

Example
*Replacing the word **input** with **feed***

```
This example illustrates the general layout of an input conveyor
offered as basic equipment.  Its function is to input products
at a suitable measured rate on to the upper level of the dispersion
section in response to the demand for more products made by the
computer scale.  Although it is possible to input products
manually directly from the manufacturing line, an input conveyor
is necessary in order to adjust the rate of product fed to the rate
of product consumed by the computer scale.
```

```
This example illustrates the general layout of a feed conveyor
offered as basic equipment.  Its function is to feed products
at a suitable measured rate on to the upper level of the dispersion
section in response to the demand for more products made by the
computer scale.  Although it is possible to feed products
manually directly from the manufacturing line, a feed conveyor
is necessary in order to adjust the rate of product fed to the rate
of product consumed by the computer scale.
```

Dear Sir/Madam

This Council has received an application under the T&C Planning Acts and Orders for

(leave 5 clear line spaces)

If you wish to see the particulars, they are available for inspection at this Department during office hours. I recognise that you, as a neighbour, may wish to comment, favourably or in the form of an objection, on this proposal. If you wish to do so, can you please reply within the next 21 days as it may not be possible to take account of objections received after this period.

Some minor applications are dealt with by officers, under delegated powers, if not more than 2 objections are lodged. However, in the event of receiving more than 2 objections, or in the event of receiving representations from your local area councillor(s), I am required to report the application to the Development Control Sub-Committee, where your views will be made known and Members will take the decision. The name(s) and address(es) of your area councillor(s) are listed overleaf. I would advise you to contact them immediately if you feel this application would affect you adversely.

Development Control Sub-Committee meetings are open to the public, should you wish to attend, and, in this event, you will be given notice of when the item containing your objects is to be considered.

May I point out that the application can only be considered on its merits in town planning terms and cannot take account of issues such as boundary disputes, land ownership or drainage, which are outside the scope of the T&C Planning Acts.

The Officer dealing with this case is _____ on Ext. ____

Yours faithfully

BOROUGH PLANNING OFFICER

Test your competence

Recall the previously stored file and make the following amendments using the find and replace facility. Store to disk and print out one copy.

Search for: T&C — Replace with: Town & Country
Search for: area — Replace with: Ward
Search for: councillor(s) — Replace with: Councillor(s)
Search for: Development Control — Replace with: DC
Search for: objections — Replace with: protests

Further practice

Please create the following as a new file and store to disk.

THE ROLE OF MENTOR WITHIN THE COLLEGE

1. Introduction

On the appointment of a new lecturer to the college, the Head of Department (or other line manager) of that new lecturer will arrange for an existing member of staff, in the new lecturers' course area, to act as a mentor or 'friend' in the early weeks of employment.

New lecturers may be experienced teachers who are new to your college, or they may be new to teaching and therefore seen as probationary teachers for at least their first year of teaching. It is the Head of Department's responsibility to inform a probationary teacher of procedures that apply during the period of probation, and for implementing these procedures.

All new staff will receive some induction, and this is the responsibility of your college Staff Development Officer.

2. The Mentor's Role

While an induction programme sets out to formally meet the needs of new lecturers, it is important in the early weeks in a new job to have easy access to some advice and support from colleagues. A new lecturer may feel very unsettled and confused, and not know where to go for help on simple, practical matters.

The idea behind a college mentor is for new lecturers to have one named person that they can ask for help from with some confidence. This could involve information on a range of issues including:

2.1 The location of rooms and facilities such as audio-visual aids and reprographics.

2.2 The system for collecting, completing and storing registers.

2.3 Access to stationery for students and staff.

2.4 The location of keys and arrangements for security of rooms and equipment.

2.5 Facilities for coffee, lunch and tea for staff etc.

The role of mentor does not preclude the kind of professional interchange that often takes place between colleagues. However, mentors should be prepared to refer new lecturers to their Heads of Department or the Staff Development Officer if they judge this to be more appropriate.

Recall and replace the word 'mentor' with 'personal adviser'
'college' with 'institution' and
'staff development officer' with 'SDO'

Check your success   Did you key in the text carefully? ☐

Did you use the 'autotab' feature to wrap text to the tab point for the numbered items? ☐

Did you recall the task successfully? ☐

Did you carry out the find and replace successfully for each request? ☐

Did you replace both Mentor with capital M and mentor with lower case m? ☐

Did you proof-read carefully? ☐

24 Moving text between pages

Edit or revise a document file by using the copy facility to move text between pages

You have already learnt in Elementary 12 how to **move** a *block* of text to a new location within a page. The same principle is applied to moving text *between pages* of a file. Markers are made at the beginning and end of the text, whether it is a sentence, a paragraph or the remainder. The text is then placed in a buffer memory using the required command. You will be required to position the cursor at the new location, either within the page or on the *next* page of the document. You then give a command to retrieve the text from the buffer memory and the text is inserted. The remaining text will move to allow for this insertion.

Edit or revise a document file by repaginating the document

Repagination occurs where a previously stored multi-page document is recalled and the page break positions are altered. It is important to ensure that the breaks occur at a sensible point so that there are no *widows* and *orphans*, eg when the first line of text or a heading appears at the bottom of a page with the accompanying text on the next page.

You will need to give a simple command to request the system to break the page at the identified point.

Example

A 2-page document might look like this before repagination. An indication has been given as to where the repagination might take place.

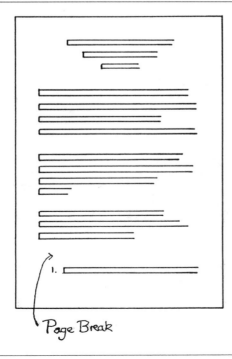

Page Break

Example

When a Homechester consultant goes to a client for the first time, there are 2 things he never takes - proposal forms or preconceived ideas.

After all, you must know what is provided for you before you can decide what arrangements you need to make for yourself.

He will then go away and think how you can plot your course in the most cost-effective and simple way.

Even within an occupational group, no 2 people are the same and his first job is to help you discover where you are now - show you what the State provides on death or retirement - and to help you focus on where you want to go in your financial life, whether it's house purchase, family protection, saving for retirement or your infant daughter's eventual wedding!

Homechester draws upon over 10 years' experience of assisting people with their financial problems.

When the consultant has set up various companies against each other to compete for your business, he will bring you what he finds to be the most suitable products for you.

Homechester will not normally charge you a fee since our income comes from the companies with whom we place your business. They pay your costs.

Homechester
Insurance and Investment
Homechester House
64 Wellington Street
EDINBURGH

MOVE TO TOP OF PAGE 1.

Homechester
Insurance and Investment
Homechester House
64 Wellington Street
EDINBURGH

Homechester draws upon over 10 years' experience of assisting people with their financial problems.

When a Homechester consultant goes to a client for the first time, there are 2 things he never takes - proposal forms or preconceived ideas.

Even within an occupational group, no 2 people are the same and his first job is to help you discover where you are now - show you what the State provides on death or retirement - and to help you focus on where you want to go in your financial life, whether it's house purchase, family protection, saving for retirement or your infant daughter's eventual wedding!

After all, you must know what is provided for you before you can decide what arrangements you need to make for yourself.

He will then go away and think how you can plot your course in the most cost-effective and simple way.

When the consultant has set up various companies against each other to compete for your business, he will bring you what he finds to be the most suitable products for you.

Homechester will not normally charge you a fee since our income comes from the companies with whom we place your business. They pay your costs.

Test your competence

Open a new document file and key in the following in *double line spacing*. Save to disk and print out one copy.

(CAPS u/s) → <u>Arranging an Exchange</u>

Home-Exchange is only an agency for the provision of information about other home exchangers. We are not responsible for the homes, the actions of the members or the accuracy of the advertised details.

<u>Initial Selection</u>   Advertisements are arranged under main headings. If you have a particular destination in mind, look at the entries and make a note of those that are of interest you. If you are more ~~free~~ flexible about where you want to go, then browse freely, noting potential exchanges. It will be to your advantage to adopt a flexible attitude. Be flexible (with both) trs regard to the timing and also the destinations.

stet   Make <u>instant</u> ~~immediate~~ ~~contan~~ contact with the people who interest you. A telephone call or airmail letter will do. These do not commit you – you are merely showing interest. More detailed correspondence will follow. When you are finally agreed that an exchange shld. take place, send a copy of the <u>Agreement Form</u> to (CAPS) your partners.

(BOLD) <u>Making the Exchange a Success</u>

1. Arrange your home so that it is easy to live in. In a loose-leaf file include:

    (a) the location of the stop-cock, fuse box, gas main controls etc.

    (b) details of how to operate the appliances and equipment in your home – central heating, washing machine, dish washer etc.

    (c) the details of when local tradesmen call

(d) a map of the local and surrounding areas

(e) the telephone number of all services (doctor, dentist, police, plumber, etc

(f) the location of useful supermarkets and shops, parks, recreational facilities etc

u/s 2. If you are <u>exchanging cars</u>, leave the car keys.

3. Ensure that a neighbour knows that an exchange is <u>happening</u> (taking place) and is prepared to be a contact.

u/s 4. Thoroughly clean cookers, fridges, cupboards and general living and sleeping areas <u>before</u> you hand over to your guests.

5. ALWAYS LEAVE THE EXCHANGE HOME AS YOU FOUND IT.

6. Leave a welcoming selection of provisions.

7. DO NOT BACK OUT OF A FIRM ARRANGEMENT BECAUSE SOMETHING BETTER TURNS UP.

HOME-EXCHANGE
9065 Pacific Avenue
Santa Cruz
CALIFORNIA 95060

} BOLD & CENTRE

RECALL THIS DRAFT AND AMEND AS INDICATED.
PRINT OUT FINAL VERSION WITH RIGHT JUSTIFICATION

BOLD + CENTRE →

ARRANGING AN EXCHANGE

Home-Exchange is only an agency for the provision of information about other home exchangers. We are not responsible for the homes, the actions of the members or the accuracy of the advertised details.

Bold
NP →

Initial Selection [Advertisements are arranged under main headings.

If you have a particular destination in mind, look at the entries and make a note of those that interest you. If you are more flexible about where you want to go, then browse freely, noting

NP

potential exchanges. [It will be to your advantage to adopt a flexible attitude. Be flexible both with regard to the timing and also the destinations.

uc + bold

uc + bold

Make immediate contact with the people who interest you. A Telephone call or airmail letter will do. These do not commit you - you are merely showing interest. More detailed correspondence will follow. When you are finally agreed that an exchange should take place, send a copy of the AGREEMENT FORM to your partners.

Making the Exchange a Success

1   Arrange your home so that it is easy to live in. In a loose-
     leaf file include:

     b
     (a)   the location of the stop-cock, fuse box, gas main
            controls etc

     c
     (b)   details of how to operate the appliances and equipment
            in your home - central heating, washing machine, dish
            washer etc

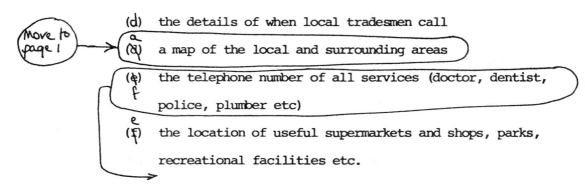

(d) the details of when local tradesmen call

~~a~~
(d) a map of the local and surrounding areas

~~(d)~~
f the telephone number of all services (doctor, dentist,

police, plumber etc)

~~e~~
(f) the location of useful supermarkets and shops, parks,

recreational facilities etc.

2   If you are <u>exchanging cars</u>, leave the car keys.

3   Ensure that a neighbour knows that an exchange is taking

place and is prepared to be a contact.

4   Thoroughly clean cookers, fridges, cupboards and general living

and sleeping areas <u>before</u> you hand over to your guests.

6
~~5~~   ALWAYS LEAVE THE EXCHANGE HOME AS YOU FOUND IT.

5
~~6~~   Leave a welcoming selection of provisions.

7   DO NOT BACK OUT OF A FIRM ARRANGEMENT BECAUSE SOMETHING

BETTER TURNS UP.

HOME-EXCHANGE

9065 Pacific Avenue

Santa Cruz

CALIFORNIA 95060

← move to top of first page

Practice from the paper

The following task has been extracted from a past PEI Examination paper. Please note that in the examination the *recalled task* will have been set up on the candidate's disk by the *tutor*. The first part of this task may therefore be prepared for you by your tutor or you may key in the document yourself.

Please key in the following text with a minimum left-hand margin of 1" (2.5 cm) and line-spacing as shown. Use a ragged right-hand margin.

TASK 1   (Candidate's Name)

THE PHARMADRUG COMPANY

TERMS OF BUSINESS
Prices

This price list replaces previous issues and is subject to change without notice. Prices charged shall be prices ruling on the date of order entry.

Payments: Payment of account is to be received by The Pharmadrug company on or before the last day of the month following month of invoice. Failure to pay on the due date will entitle (thecompany) to withhold delivery of subsequent (a) orders.

(Breakeages:) Goods should be signed for as 'unexamined' and any shortage or damage must be reported in writing within 3 days of delivery to both the Head (office) of the company and the Carriers, otherwise no claim can be considered. The complete packaging should be retained if pilfering is suspected or if breakage has occurred. If pilfering is suspected the company and the Carriers should be notified immediately.

Non-Delivery:

In the event of non-arrival of goods, customers must inform The Pharmadrug Company within 7 days of the date of the invoice or advice of despatch, otherwise no claim can be considered.

SPECIALIST TEACHER PLEASE NOTE

To aid your preparation some "deliberate mistakes" are circled and care should be taken to ensure that errors are repeated. These errors will be indicated on the candidate's paper.

The examination requires you to recall the stored **draft** which will have been keyed in by your **tutor** and follow the instructions given on the *word processing request form*.
This particular task tests the following competences:

Checklist reference 17	extracting work details from job sheet
Checklist reference 18	altering margins and line spacing
Checklist reference 20.2	keying in text from manuscript
Checklist reference 22	using right margin justification
Checklist reference 19	using the display features
Checklist references 9, 10, 21	using basic editing skills – insert, delete, etc
Checklist reference 12	using the move facility
Checklist reference 21.1	business document – report
Checklist reference 26.2	presentation of document

WORD PROCESSING REQUEST FORM

Task number: ...1......   Author's name: .L. Warren...........

Create a document: ..... New document name: ....

Edit a document: .✓..... Existing document name: ....

Rename document as: ....

Standard paragraphs are stored as:

....

....

....

Type of copy: Draft: .... Final: .✓...............

Line spacing: 1 .... 2 .... As copy: .✓...........

No of copies required: .1...............................

Paper size: A4 ..✓... A5 ..... Portrait: .✓... Landscape: .....

Date required: .... Retain on file: .... Delete: ....

SPECIAL INSTRUCTIONS:

JUSTIFY RT. MARGIN
All headings, except the main heading, to be
paragraph headings
Company with an initial cap. throughout.

THE PHARMADRUG COMPANY ← *(Centre & embolden)*

(line clear)
(line space)
TERMS OF BUSINESS ← *(centre)*

Prices *caps*

This price list replaces previous issues and is subject to change without notice. ¶
~~Prices charged shall be prices ruling on the date of order entry.~~

Payments: Payment of account is to be received by The Pharmadrug company on or before the last day of the month following month of invoice. Failure to pay ~~on~~ ⋀ *by this* ~~the due date~~ will entitle the company to withhold delivery of subsequent ~~a~~ orders. ¶ *date*

⋀ # ¶ Breakages: Goods should be signed for as 'unexamined' and any (shortage or) *trs* [damage must be reported in writing within 3 days of delivery to both the Head *u c* office of the company and the Carriers, otherwise no claim can be considered. [The *N P* complete packaging should be retained if pilfering is suspected or if breakage has occurred. If pilfering is suspected the company and the Carriers should be notified immediately.

(Move to Ⓐ)

Non-Delivery: *(failure of goods to arrive)*

In the event of ~~non-arrival of goods~~, customers must inform The Pharmadrug *⋀ one* Company within ~~7 days~~ of the date of the invoice or advice of despatch, otherwise *week* no claim can be considered.

Carriage: All orders must be placed in accordance w. the Pharmadrug Company Delivery Schedule and these will be despatched by the most appropriate route, carriage paid. ~~We~~ Where a customer suggests an alternative route or places an order outside the normal schedule, The Pharmadrug Co. shall have the right to charge the entire cost of delivery, irrespective of the value of the order.

Deliveries: Every effort wl. be made to supply orders promptly but the company will not accept responsibility for suspension or delay in deliveries nor for the consequences thereof.

Returned Goods:

Goods are not supplied on 'sale or return basis'. Returns which must be in whole original packs supplied directly by the company wl. be accepted only w. the prior written permission of the co..

Credit will normally be allowed on authorised returns as follows:

indent 1" (2.5cm) from margin

(a) Goods authorised for return within 14 days of despatch – 100% allowance

b) Initial stocks of new products returned within one year of launch – 100% allowance

(c) Any other goods – no allowance

double-line spacing

General : The above conditions shall apply to all total orders for goods rec'd by the Company for supply in the United Kingdom.

Ⓐ

TELEPHONE ORDERS (retain shoulder heading)

Orders for our products may be placed by telephoning 032 417 926 ext. 4801. Outside office hours callers shd. use the order recording service.

Check your success

Did you read the request form carefully? ☐

Did you follow the instruction to use double spacing? ☐

Did you indent the section from the left margin? ☐

Did you move 'A' correctly? ☐

Did you insert the paragraph successfully? ☐

Did you *embolden and centre* the heading? ☐

Did you *edit* the document as instructed – insertions, deletions, new paragraphs, etc? ☐

Did you search for all instances of 'company' and change them to 'Company'? ☐

Did you repaginate the document appropriately? ☐

Did you proof-read carefully? ☐

Did you print out with *right justification*? ☐

25 Standard paragraphs

Assemble a document from previously stored standard paragraphs and key in variable information at in-fill points as required

The term **boilerplating** is often used to describe the facility whereby standard paragraphs are stored on the system, either within a library document facility or as separate files, and then *selected* paragraphs are merged together to form *one new file*.

The standard paragraphs can contain **in-fill** points which are completed with **variable information** in the same way as in standard forms. You have already covered this at Elementary level. Please refer to Section 14 if necessary.

In the Intermediate examination the standard paragraphs will have been set up previously on the system by the specialist teacher and you have a printed copy in your examination paper. You will be required to create 2 separate documents by boilerplating or **merging** different combinations of these previously stored paragraphs, as indicated in the *Special Instructions* of the Word Processing Request Form.

Example
Standard paragraphs

<u>Standard Paragraphs</u>

1   We enclose our account for the sum of @———— *in-fill symbols*

2   We have not received a reply to our invoice dated @ and assume that this is simply an oversight on your part.

3   Despite several reminders you have still failed to settle your account, reference @. We must insist that you settle within 7 days.

4   Your account with us is now @ months overdue and we urgently require payment by return of post. You will appreciate that our extremely competitive prices are based on the assumption that accounts will be settled promptly.

5   Your repeated failure to settle promptly means that we must seriously consider withdrawing the privilege of trade discount in future.

Standard
Para

Dear Mr Chou

1 We enclose our account for the sum
of £156.   in fill

4 Despite several reminders you have
still failed to settle your account,
reference XZ3297. We must insist
that you/settle within 7 days.
in fill

6 Your repeated failure to settle
promptly means that we must seriously
consider withdrawing the privilege
of trade discount in future.

Yours sincerely

Accounts Manager

Standard
Para

Dear Mr Saijo

in-fill

2 We have not received/a reply to our
invoice dated 29 October and assume
this is simply an oversight on your
part.

in-fill

5 Your account with us is now 2 months
overdue and we urgently require
payment by return of post. You will
appreciate that our extremely
competitive prices are based on the
assumption that accounts will be
settled promptly.

Yours sincerely

Accounts Manager

**Test your
competence**

Either ask your tutor, or key in yourself, the following paragraphs, as *separate files*, or
using a *library document facility*. Do not type headings 'Standard Paragraph 1', etc. Use
a minimum left-hand margin of 1"/2.5 cm.

Standard Paragraph 1

M E M O R A N D U M

FROM: David Ludberry, Sales Manager   REF: DL/@

TO: @   DATE: @

Standard Paragraph 2

Thank you for your memo confirming that you will be attending the @
Meeting at the @ on @.

Standard Paragraph 3

The Company is holding a series of meetings at several locations
around the country. The objective of these meetings is to give @ an
opportunity to meet some of the Directors and ask questions.

Standard Paragraph 4

The Company is holding a special meeting at Head Office to give @ an
opportunity to meet some of the Directors and Senior Management and
ask questions.

Using the standard paragraphs which have been previously stored either as *separate files* or within a *library facility*, create **2** memos to the representatives.

The memorandum heading is contained in the first paragraph.

Insert today's date and add your initials to the reference.

1 Steve Bacon   Infills, Para 2: North East Regional
George Hotel, Harrogate
Monday 8 September 19–

                                         Para 3: Representatives

2 Tim Wilde   Infills, Para 2: South East Regional
Midland Hotel, Norwich
Wed 10 Sept 19–

                                         Para 3: New representatives

Note to the Specialist Teacher

The following paragraphs need to be keyed in so that candidates can recall them to produce standard letters. If your system has a library document facility then they can be typed into this. If no such facility exists, please key them into separate files.

Please key in either with <u>enter</u> points or by inserting code symbols eg & or @ to indicate the enter points.

TASK 2   (Candidate's Name)

STANDARD PARAGRAPH 1

FACSIMILE TRANSMISSION SHEET.

IF YOU DO NOT RECEIVE ALL OF THIS FAX
PLEASE TELEPHONE 032 417926 IMMEDIATELY

TO: @

FAX NO: @

FROM: Marketing Director

DATE: (Today's date)

NO OF COPIES (including this page): 1

SUBJECT: <u>PROPOSED NATIONAL SALES MEETING - LONDON</u>

You will be receiving a copy of the Programme for the above meeting in the next few days.

STANDARD PARAGRAPH 2

Please be prepared to give a short talk @ about your team's success with @. If you require us to prepare slides for you contact Jan Hughes at Head Office.

STANDARD PARAGRAPH 3

It is proposed that you should lead a discussion group @ on @. Could you let me have your ideas.

STANDARD PARAGRAPH 4

You will be required to hold a follow-up meeting with your team within two weeks of the Meeting. @ from Head Office will attend this meeting.

WORD PROCESSING REQUEST FORM

Task number: ..2...... Author's name: ..L.Warren.............

Create a document: ..✓.. New document name: ....

Edit a document: .... Existing document name: ....

Rename document as: ....

Standard paragraphs are stored as:

①.................... ②....................
③.................... ④....................

....

Type of copy: Draft: .... Final: ...✓.............

Line spacing: 1 ..✓....... 2 .... As copy: ....

No of copies required: .1.of.each.........................

Paper size: A4 .✓... A5 ..... Portrait: ..✓... Landscape: .....

Date required: .Today.... Retain on file: .✓.. Delete: ....

SPECIAL INSTRUCTIONS:

Fax 1   David Williams   Fax 2
         Northern Regional Manager
         0964 31724   Sandra Scott
         on the first day   Southern Regional Manager
         Allvax   0477 6194
         Brian Lewis   on the second day
         Paras 1, 2, 4.   Ditrex
                                            Lesley Smith
                                            Paras 1, 3, 4

Check your success   Did you successfully create 2 faxes from the correct standard paragraphs?   ☐

Did you successfully in-fill the variable information?   ☐

Did you use today's date?   ☐

Did you print out one copy of each fax?   ☐

26 Intermediate examination questions

There now follows an Intermediate Examination paper which has been worked through and solutions provided.

If you wish, you may work through the paper yourself before comparing your printouts with the solutions provided.

In order to 'mirror' examination conditions it will be necessary for your *Specialist Teacher* to set up those tasks which need to be stored on disk prior to the commencement of the examination paper.

Further practice

For further practice, copies of past papers can be obtained from PEI. It is suggested that you practise working through as many papers as you can before taking the examination.

Note: For further helpful hints, *see* **Section 35 Preparing for the Word Processing examinations**.

This paper must be returned
with the candidates' work.
Failure to do so will result in
delay in processing the
candidates' scripts

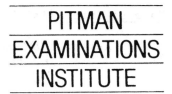

WORD PROCESSING - INTERMEDIATE

To be handed to Specialist Teacher before the date of the examination

This pack contains:

*One Specialist Teacher's instructions
and details of Tasks to be created on
storage medium.*

1   In advance of the date of the examination, you are asked to create documents on the storage medium for the attached tasks.

2   You may key in text using character line length for any appropriate pitch.

3   With the exception of line endings, which may vary with the choice of pitch, please follow the text <u>exactly</u> (including "deliberate mistakes").

4   Copies of these documents should be created on the storage medium for the exclusive use of each individual candidate.

5   <u>Print out a copy of your work to be attached to the Attestation Form for the examination</u>.

6   Because word processing systems vary so widely between Centres it is not possible for the Examiner to specify file names for documents. Please allocate suitable file names for the documents created (TASK 1, TASK 2, etc are suggested, as appropriate). Likewise, please devise suitable file names for candidates to store their completed tasks.

7   Please complete the spaces provided on each of the WORD PROCESSING REQUEST FORMS, or as otherwise indicated, so that these file names will be available to candidates at the start of the examination.

8   The preparation of all examination material must be regarded as strictly confidential and should be carried out under the supervision of the Invigilator. No details of the content of the examination may be divulged, and the Specialist Teacher and Invigilator are asked to sign the Attestation Form to this effect. This should be enclosed with the worked scripts, together with a printed specimen copy of each of the prepared tasks.

9   All material must be erased from the system and storage medium at the end of the examination after the completion of all the required printing.

_Please key in the following text with a minimum left-hand margin of 1"
(2.5 cm) and line-spacing as shown. Use a ragged RH margin._

TASK 2   (Candidate's Name)

Flower Arranging

It is important that you have the correct tools and equipment when arranging
flowers. There is nothing worse than finding you are short of something
when you are halfway through an arrangement. Your hobby does not seem so
expensive when you first begin if you start with just one or two basic tools
and add to them.

SCISSORS

There are several very good makes available and it is up to you to find ones
that are of a suitable size and weight for you. Make sure that the rings
are comfortable and do not trap your fingers. We recommend the Walker and
Trapp-Ribbon ranges as being of medium cost.

SECATEURS

These will be necessary when you wish to cut heavy stems of plant material
or wire.

KNIFE

A sharp knife is essential. It can be used for trimming all kinds of stems,
removing thorns and leaves from stems and for cutting floral foam.

FLORAL FOAM

There are two main types - green for using with fresh flowers, pale brown
for using with dried and fabric flowers. The green type must be thoroughly
soaked before use.

The foam comes in many shapes and sizes - bricks, cylinders, squares, etc.
All shapes can be cut to the appropriate sizes. We stock a full range.

FOAM-FIX

This is a dark green substance similar to modelling clay which will stick
almost any dry surfaces together.

TASK 3   (Candidate's Name)

<u>STANDARD PARAGRAPH 1</u>

Ref MG/(your initials)

Today's date

&

Dear &

Thank you for your order of &.

<u>STANDARD PARAGRAPH 2</u>

I regret that we are currently out of stock of &. However, this will be despatched to you within & weeks.

<u>STANDARD PARAGRAPH 3</u>

Your order is enclosed.

<u>STANDARD PARAGRAPH 4</u>

We are pleased to enclose a copy of our current brochure which contains many special offers. May I draw your attention to pages 45 and 46 where details of free gifts according to the value of your order are itemised.

We look forward to your continued custom.

Yours sincerely
GREENSDALE GARDEN CENTRE

Martin Greensdale

Enc

Please key in the following text with a minimum left-hand margin of 1"
(2.5 cm) and line-spacing as shown

TASK 4   (Candidate's Name)

MEMORANDUM

TO

FROM

DATE

Leave 4 clear line spaces

GGC - EXPANTION PLANS

I am pleased to be able to bring to your attention the following planns for
GGC which shows the confidance that our Directors have in the future of the
buisness. I am pleased to to be able to tell you that the company is
planning a period of expansion.

I should like to congratulate the above managers ontheir promotoin to the
above projects. I wish them well in their endeavours

As you are aware, the centre will be undergoing dramatic changes. I hope
that everyone will help to make it as easy as possible.

These changes should ensure that GGC remains the best garden centre in teh
region.

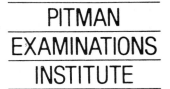

WORD PROCESSING - INTERMEDIATE

This paper must be returned with the candidate's work, otherwise the entry will be void and no result will be issued.

No.

PITMAN EXAMINATIONS INSTITUTE

CANDIDATE'S NAME ....

(Block letters please)

CENTRE NO. ....DATE ....

This examination lasts for 1 hour and 30 minutes and consists of four tasks which you should file on the storage medium for printing out later. The Invigilator will give you instructions about arrangements for printing out your documents.

You have 10 minutes to read through the tasks and documents before starting the examination. Check that you have been given all the document names required to create, recall or store your finished work.

———————————

FOR EXAMINER'S USE ONLY

COMPLETION	ACCURACY	DISPLAY

You work as a secretary to Martin Greensdale, Manager of Greensdale Garden Centre. Each day your in-tray contains a mixture of new tasks and amended documents returned by Mr Greensdale.

Carry out the tasks attached, following any instructions given on the standard Word Processing Request Forms or on the documents themselves. Take care to proof-read and correct any errors.

You may carry out the tasks in any order you think appropriate. However, please collate the printouts in the correct sequence.

WORD PROCESSING REQUEST FORM

Task number: .!..	Author's name: .M.Greensdale..........

Create a document: ✓... New document name: ....

Edit a document: .... Existing document name: ....

Rename document as: ....

Standard paragraphs are stored as: ....

....

Type of copy: Draft: .... Final: ✓...

Line spacing: 1 .... 2 .... As copy: ✓...

No of copies required: ...!......

Paper size: A4 ✓... A5 .... Portrait: ✓... Landscape: ...

Date required: ..asap....... Retain on file: ✓... Delete: ......

SPECIAL INSTRUCTIONS:

Please key-in the attached
documents and print one copy.
Please ensure that this fits on
one side of A4 paper.

GREENSDALE ↙ (spaced caps) ⎫ centre
Garden Centre of the Year ⎬ both lines

THURSDAY EVENING EVENTS CALENDAR ← (Bold)
7.00 PM TO 8.30 PM - ALL WELCOME - ALL FREE

MAY
Thursday, 3rd   Hanging Basket Demonstration - Sarah
Tothill Representative from PRT Compost
(Compost for Hanging Baskets)

JUNE
Thursday, 14th   Barbecue Demonstration - Soroco Barbecues
Representative from Mela - Advice on
Garden Furniture
Barbecue Cooking - Maria Rodriguez

JULY
Thursday, 12th   Water Gardening - Tony Parker
Ponds, Pumps, Plants, Fish

AUGUST
Thursday, 9th   Conservatories - Advantages,
Disadvantages, Styles - Bob West
Plants for Conservatories and
Patios — Suma Patel

SEPTEMBER
Thursday, 13th   Spring Flowering Bulbs - Tony Parker - Representative
from PRT Compost (Compost for Bulbs)

OCTOBER
Thursday, 11th   Display of Fireworks

(continued)

NOVEMBER
Thursday, 5th   Floral Art Demonstration - Martha Pierce
                 Arranging House Plants - Michael Farmer

The centre is open every day from 9.00 am
to 8.00 pm throughout December and has
some of the finest decorations on display
in the country.

WORD PROCESSING REQUEST FORM

Task number: .2.	Author's name: M. Greensdale

Create a document: ....   New document name: ....

Edit a document: ✓...   Existing document name: ....

Rename document as: ....

Standard paragraphs are stored as: ....

. . . .

Type of copy: Draft: ....   Final: .✓..

Line spacing: 1 .✓..   2 ....   As copy: ....

No of copies required: ...!......

Paper size: A4 .✓..   A5 ....   Portrait: ....   Landscape: ...

Date required: ..asap.......   Retain on file: .✓.. Delete: ......

SPECIAL INSTRUCTIONS:

Please complete the attached
work and print one copy.
Repaginate as appropriate.

TASK 2   (Candidate's Name)

Flower Arranging ← caps   Please justify right margin

leave 2 line spaces

It is important that you have the correct tools and equipment when arranging
flowers. There is nothing worse than finding you are short of something that
when you are halfway through an arrangement. Your hobby does not seem is not quite so
expensive when you first begin, if you start with just one or two basic tools
and add to them.

SCISSORS
                                                you must choose ones

stet   There are several very good makes available and it is up to you to find ones
that are of a suitable size and weight for you. Make sure that the rings
are comfortable and do not trap your fingers. We recommend the Walker and
Trapp Ribbon ranges as being of medium cost.

SECATEURS

These will be necessary when you wish to cut heavy stems of plant material
or wire.

move to *
KNIFE

A sharp knife is essential. It can be used for trimming all kinds of stems,
removing thorns and leaves from stems and for cutting floral foam.   This
need not cost a lot of money.

FLORAL FOAM

There are two main types - green for using with fresh flowers, pale brown
for using with dried and fabric flowers. The green type must be thoroughly
soaked before use.

The foam comes in many shapes and sizes - bricks, cylinders, squares, etc.
All shapes can be cut to the appropriate sizes. We stock a full range.

FOAM-FIX
                              in texture and appearance
This is a dark green substance similar to modelling clay which will stick
almost any dry surfaces together.

ADHESIVE TAPE

This may be used for securely fixing the
foam to the container especially in
large designs. You must make sure that
the surface is completely dry.

(continued)

WATERING CAN

Leave 2" (5.0cm) for the complete paragraph

This item is quite indispensable. Even Though you hv. soaked the foam beforehand, evaporation wl. take place. You must never let the foam dry out. The size you choose wl. depend on you — try to choose one that is neither too small nor too large. One That holds 3 pints (1.5 Litres) is probably ideal.

SPRAY

This is v. handy for giving yr. arrangement a final spray to make the plants last as long as possible. You shd. also give the flowers a daily spray in addition to watering Them.

*

indent 1" (2.5cm) from both margins

Remember to browse Through the items in our extensive display of equipment for flower arrangers. Our stocks are usually complete but, if you cannot find what you need, please ask at the Information Desk

WORD PROCESSING REQUEST FORM

Task number: 3.	Author's name: MG

Create a documents ✔   New document name: ....

Edit a document: ....   Existing document name: ....

Rename document as: ....

Standard paragraphs are stored as: ....

....

Type of copy:	Draft:	Final: ✔	

Line spacing: 1 ✔   2 ....   As copy: ....

No of copies required: 1 of each

Paper size: A4 ✔   A5 ....   Portrait: ✔   Landscape: ...

Date required: today   Retain on file: ✔   Delete: ......

SPECIAL INSTRUCTIONS:

Please use the standard paragraphs stored
on disk and send the following letters:

mr T Gardner
14 Elm Tree Close
BRIGHOUSE
HD4 3LM

mr T Shah
27 The Poplars
HUDDERSFIELD
HD4 3NR

Order date = 16 September
Out of Stock = Cymbidium
No of weeks = 4
Paras 1, 2, 4

Order date = 18 September

Paras 1, 3, 4

(NB A hardcopy of the standard
paragraphs is attached for
reference only.)

This is a hard copy of the standard paragraphs stored on disk and is for reference only.

<u>TASK 3</u>   (Candidate's Name)

<u>STANDARD PARAGRAPH 1</u>

Ref MG/(your initials)

Today's date

&

Dear &

Thank you for your order of &.

<u>STANDARD PARAGRAPH 2</u>

I regret that we are currently out of stock of &. However, this will be despatched to you within & weeks.

<u>STANDARD PARAGRAPH 3</u>

Your order is enclosed.

<u>STANDARD PARAGRAPH 4</u>

We are pleased to enclose a copy of our current brochure which contains many special offers. May I draw your attention to pages 45 and 46 where details of free gifts according to the value of your order are itemised.

We look forward to your continued custom.

Yours sincerely
GREENSDALE GARDEN CENTRE

Martin Greensdale

Enc

WORD PROCESSING REQUEST FORM

Task number: .4.   Author's name: ...MG..........................

Create a document: ....   New document name: ....

Edit a document: .✓..   Existing document name: ....

                           Rename document as: ....

Standard paragraphs are stored as: ....

....

Type of copy: Draft: ....   Final: ✓...

Line spacing: 1 ....   2 ....   As copy: ✓..

No of copies required: ....1..

Paper size: A4 .✓..   A5 ....   Portrait: .✓..   Landscape: ...

Date required: ...Today......   Retain on file: .✓.. Delete: ......

SPECIAL INSTRUCTIONS:

Our Junior typed the attached and hasn't corrected the errors. Please will you correct it and print me a copy with my additional amendments.

Put GGC as Greensdale Garden centre with initial caps, please.

TASK 4   (Candidate's Name)

MEMORANDUM

TO All Staff

FROM M Greensdale

DATE (today)

↑↓ (Leave only 2 clear lines here)

GGC - EXPANTION PLANS

I am pleased to be able to bring to your attention the following plamns for
GGC which shows the confidance that our Directors have in the future of the
NP buisness. [I am pleased to to be able to tell you that the company is
planning a period of expansion.

I should like to congratulate the above managers ontheir promotoin to the
above projects. I wish them well in their endeavours

As you are aware, the centre will be undergoing dramatic changes. I hope ⁋
that everyone will help to make it as easy as possible.
        have been made to
These changes should ensure that GGC remains the best garden centre in teh
region.

MONTH OF COMPLETION	PROJECT	MANAGER
June	Water Garden	G Adams
September	Conservatories	M Parker
November	Floral Art Section	A Rowe
December	Container /Statuary	M Shah

double line spacing

whilst the major bldg. + re structuring is
taking place, I appreciate th. there wl. be
extra work in order to ensure th. the customers
are not inconvenienced. I am sure that
you will do all that you can to help.

In the first instance we will
organise the centre:

(continued)

indent at least 5 clear spaces from left margin

cut flowers move to reception
books + gifts move to west counter area
house plants move to south room
pots move to the position
vacated by cut flowers.

Martin Harris will produce a schedule
of times + persons involved. Please
assist him in every way you can.

———————————

Worked solutions

TASK 1   (Candidate's Name)

                    G R E E N S D A L E
                 Garden Centre of the Year

THURSDAY EVENING EVENTS CALENDAR
7.00 PM TO 8.30 PM - ALL WELCOME - ALL FREE

MAY

Thursday, 3rd   Hanging Basket Demonstration - Sarah Tothill
                       Representative from PRT Compost (Compost for
                       Hanging Baskets)

JUNE

Thursday, 14th   Barbecue Demonstration - Soroco Barbecues
                       Representative from Mela - Advice on Garden
                       Furniture
                       Barbecue Cooking - Maria Rodriguez

JULY

Thursday, 12th   Water Gardening - Tony Parker
                       Ponds, Pumps, Plants, Fish

AUGUST

Thursday, 9th   Conservatories - Advantages, Disadvantages,
                       Styles - Bob West
                       Plants for Conservatories and Patios - Suma
                       Patel

SEPTEMBER

Thursday, 13th   Spring Flowering Bulbs - Tony Parker -
                       Representative from PRT Compost (Compost for
                       Bulbs)

OCTOBER

Thursday, 11th   Display of Fireworks

NOVEMBER

Thursday, 5th   Floral Art Demonstration - Martha Pierce
                       Arranging House Plants - Michael Farmer

The Centre is open every day from 9.00 am to 8.00 pm throughout
December and has some of the finest decorations on display in the
country.

TASK 2   (Candidate's Name)

FLOWER ARRANGING

It is important that you have the correct tools and equipment
when arranging flowers. There is nothing worse than finding that
you are short of something when you are halfway through an
arrangement. Your hobby is not quite so expensive when you first
begin, if you start with just one or two basic tools and add to
them.

SCISSORS

There are several very good makes available and you must choose
ones that are of a suitable size and weight for you. Make sure
that the rings are comfortable and do not trap your fingers.

SECATEURS

These will be necessary to cut heavy stems of plant material or
wire.

FLORAL FOAM

There are two main types - green for using with fresh flowers,
pale brown for using with fabric and dried flowers. The green
type must be soaked before use. The foam comes in many shapes
and sizes - bricks, cylinders, squares etc. All shapes can be
cut to the appropriate size. We stock a full range.

ADHESIVE TAPE

This may be used for securely fixing the foam to the container
especially in large designs. You must make sure that the surface
is completely dry.

FOAM-FIX

This is a dark green substance similar in texture and appearance
to modelling clay which will stick almost any dry surfaces
together.

WATERING CAN

                    This item is quite indispensable. Even
                    though you have soaked the foam beforehand,
                    evaporation will take place. You must never
                    let the foam dry out. The size you choose
                    will depend on you - try to choose one that
                    is neither too small nor too large. One that
                    holds 3 pints (1.5 litres) is probably ideal.

SPRAY

This is very handy for giving your arrangement a final spray to
make the plants last as long as possible. You should also give
the flowers a daily spray in addition to watering them.

KNIFE

A sharp knife is essential. It can be used for trimming all
kinds of stems, removing thorns and leaves from stems and for
cutting floral foam. This need not cost a lot of money.

> Remember to browse through the items in our
> extensive display of equipment for flower
> arrangers. Our stocks are usually complete
> but, if you cannot find what you need,
> please ask at the Information Desk.

TASK 3   (Candidate's Name)

Ref MG/aa

13 October 1992

Mr T Gardner
14 Elm Tree Close
BRIGHOUSE
HD4 3LM

Dear Mr Gardner

Thank you for your order of 16 September.

I regret that we are currently out of stock of Cymbidium.
However, this will be despatched to you within 4 weeks.

We are pleased to enclose a copy of our current brochure which
contains many special offers. May I draw your attention to pages
45 and 46 where details of free gifts according to the value of
your order are itemised.

We look forward to your continued custom.

Yours sincerely
GREENSDALE GARDEN CENTRE

Martin Greensdale

Enc

Ref MG/aa

13 October 1992

Mr T Shah
27 The Poplars
HUDDERSFIELD
HD4 3NR

Dear Mr Shah

Thank you for your order of 18 September.

Your order is enclosed.

We are pleased to enclose a copy of our current brochure which
contains many special offers. May I draw your attention to pages
45 and 46 where details of free gifts according to the value of
your order are itemised.

We look forward to your continued custom.

Yours sincerely
GREENSDALE GARDEN CENTRE

Martin Greensdale

Enc

MEMORANDUM

TO   All Staff

FROM   M Greensdale

DATE   13 October 1992

Greensdale Garden Centre - EXPANSION PLANS

I am pleased to be able to bring to your attention the following
plans for Greensdale Garden Centre which shows the confidence
that our Directors have in the future of the business.

I am pleased to be able to tell you that the company is planning
a period of expansion.

MONTH OF COMPLETION	PROJECT	MANAGER
June	Water Garden	G Adams
September	Conservatories	M Parker
November	Floral Art Section	A Rowe
December	Container/Statuary	M Shah

I should like to congratulate the above managers on their
promotion to the above projects. I wish them well in their
endeavours.

These changes have been made to ensure that Greensdale Garden
Centre remains the best garden centre in the region.

Whilst the major building and restructuring is taking place, I
appreciate that there will be extra work in order to ensure that
the customers are not inconvenienced. I am sure that you will do
all that you can to help.

In the first instance we will organise the centre:

        cut flowers move to reception
        books and gifts move to west counter area
        house plants move to south room
        pots move to the position vacated by cut flowers.

Martin Harris will produce a schedule of times and persons
involved. Please assist him in every way you can.

Part 3 **Advanced**

Instructions for Part 3

If you have already acquired word processing skills at Intermediate level, either by completing the first two parts of this guide or through practical experience in the workplace, then you will find the following break-down of the competences required to be successful in the **Advanced Word Processing** examination appropriate to your needs.

The same approach as in Parts 1 and 2 has been adopted whereby a skill is firstly *identified*, then *practised* using example material and material from a past PEI examination paper, and then assessed. The areas of knowledge and skills to be achieved follow the sequence set out in the **checklist**.

You are advised to maintain a **portfolio** of your work with a copy of the **checklist** for recording your progress.

Syllabus

Word Processing – Advanced

(Time allowed – 2 hours excluding printing time, plus 10 minutes for reading.)

Aim

The aim of the examination is to test the candidate's ability to use a word processor to prepare, process and present realistic business documents with the speed and accuracy which satisfy the assessment criteria.

Target population

The examination is for the person aiming for employment as a word processor operator, capable of using the full range of word processing functions and working without supervision. Such a person should have a good command of English language, a sound knowledge of office systems and the conventions for the display of business documents. He or she should show initiative in the interpretation of tasks.

Objectives

In addition to those objectives stated in the Word Processing Intermediate syllabus, the candidate should be able to:

1 **Create documents**
These could include:

   – a form or tear-off slip
   – and an item of display

2 **Edit documents**
copy text between pages

identify and correct inconsistencies of style within the text, eg figures, times, dates and measurements

3 **Set/amend layout**
use the tabulation facility to produce tables **with horizontal ruling**, indented text and leaving space of a specified size

use headers, footers and page numbering

4 **Assemble, complete or merge standard documents**
insert items of information extracted from an existing task

create a standard document and merge it with specified records or an existing data file

5 **Proof-read and correct documents**
identify and correct "deliberate" mistakes of grammar, spelling, punctuation and typewriting **in identified tasks in both typescript and manuscript**, without reference to the correct copy

6 **Print documents**
print documents on either single sheet or continuous stationery in an acceptable format **on portrait OR landscape paper**

The examination

The examination will consist of 4 in-tray assignments and the candidate will be assumed to be working in one organisation. Each examination will contain both (a) text to be created and stored, and (b) text to be retrieved for revision. The candidate will be judged on the quality of the printed output he or she produces.

The printing of documents during the examination may be carried out at the discretion of the candidates and the Centre.

Assessment

Candidates' performance will be assessed on the criteria of accuracy, presentation and production rate.

To achieve a **Pass** grade, candidates must complete all tasks and must attain a 98.5% standard of accuracy with no more than 8 presentation errors.

A **First Class Pass** will be awarded if candidates achieve a 99% standard of accuracy with no more than 4 presentation errors.

Administration

Prior to the examination, the Specialist Teacher will be expected to prepare and store documents or part documents to be recalled by the candidates during the examination. The Specialist Teacher will also be responsible for assigning names to each candidate's documents and notes about this will accompany the set of papers. At the end of the printing the Specialist Teacher must erase all files from the storage media.

Checklist – Advanced

			Aided	Date	Unaided	Date
27	**Advanced display**					
27.1	Create form or tear-off slip and an item of display					
27.2	Produce a table with horizontal ruling and print on A4 landscape paper					
28	**Further editing**					
	Headers, footers and page numbering					
	Insert an item extracted from a previous task					
	Identify and correct inconsistencies of style					
	Identify and correct 'deliberate' mistakes in both typescript and manuscript					
	Copy text between pages					
29	**Mail merge**					
	Create a standard document					
	Merge it with specified records or an existing datafile					
30	**Advanced examination questions**					
	Ensure that all competences learned in Part 3 meet the required standard for the Advanced examination					

27 Advanced display

Create a form or tear-off slip and an item of display
Produce a table with horizontal ruling and print on A4 landscape paper

In the PEI Advanced Word Processing Examination you will be expected to be able to create a variety of documents including **forms** and **tear-off slips**. It is not expected that you will draw the broken line on these through the margins to both edges of the paper. This is difficult to achieve and so it is quite acceptable to draw the tear-off line from margin to margin.

It is expected that you will be able to draw up a **table** which will include **horizontal ruling**. This can be done with the underscore key. The tables will usually be set so that they display more attractively on A4 landscape paper, though it is quite acceptable for you to reduce the spaces between columns in order for the text to fit on A4 portrait paper.

To calculate the margins that you need on **A4 landscape paper**, the paper measures 11.66" (29.7 cm). This means that you can type 140 characters in 12 pitch or 116 characters in 10 pitch from edge to edge. You can then choose your margins accordingly. A ruler line of 100 characters (8.3") in 12 pitch or 96 characters (9.6") in 10 pitch leaves sensible margins, though you must choose your own margins depending on the material to be displayed. If you work in point size and fonts other than Courier you must plan carefully. Remember that proportional spaced fonts often appear to be out of alignment on the screen.

Whenever you are typing material in **columns**, you should set tab stops and this is imperative in proportionally spaced typefaces.

Some material will involve the use of **decimal tab stops** – remember that figures centre along the decimal point and you will need to take account of this and set the decimal tab at the decimal point.

Example

INCOME AND EXPENDITURE FOR CLARKTON COMPANY

FINANCIAL YEAR ENDING 31 MARCH 19--

INCOME	£'000	EXPENDITURE	£'000
Sales	654.4	Salaries	475.2
Rent	3.1	Administration	89.3
Stock in warehouse A	67.3	Heating and lighting	6.9
		Net profit	153.4
	————		————
Total	724.8	Total	724.8

The above account has been presented as a summary. For more detailed information please contact the Accountant, Alice Barker.

Create a new file using a suitable file name and key in the following.
Save the file to disk and print out one copy.

DAY TRIP TO CRYSTAL FACTORY ← Centre e u/c

SATURDAY 23 JUNE } Centre

COST $12.50

By popular demand we are making another trip to the Chrystal Factory and will be combining it with a visit to one of the local garden centres.

The coach will depart from the Admin Building at 0800 hrs and the itinerary is as below:

DEPARTURE

0800 Leave Admin Building
0930 Arrive at motorway service centre for morning coffee
1000 Arrive at Chrystal Factory
1200 Lunch in factory Restaurant
1330 Leave Factory for Garden Centre
1415 Arrive at Garden Centre

RETURN

1630 Leave Garden Centre
1700 Brief stop for tea
1900 Arrival back

Please reserve - - - - seats for me on the Crystal Factory trip. I enclose a cheque for - - - - - .

Name - - - -
Address - - -
Return to: Ms P Nash, Administration, Berretts, Crown Way, Auckland.

Check your success
Did you centre all headings? ☐

Did you underscore the main heading? ☐

Did you expand Admin and hrs? ☐

Did you correct the misspellings of crystal? ☐

Did you draw the horizontal line and the dashed line? ☐

Did you use the underscore or full stop for the items in the tear-off slip? ☐

Did you draw these lines the full width? ☐

Did you print on landscape paper? ☐

Practice from the paper

The following task, extracted from a past paper, tests these competences:

Checklist reference 17   extracting work details from the job sheet
Checklist reference 19   using display features
Checklist reference 21.2   expanding abbreviations
Checklist reference 27.2   displaying material in columns, drawing horizontal lines and printing on landscape paper

---

WORD PROCESSING REQUEST FORM

Task number: ..1..	Author's name: ..M.M................................
Create a document: ..✓...	New document name: ....
Edit a document:	Existing document name: ....
Datafile:	Rename document as: ....
Standard paragraphs are stored as:	
Type of copy: Draft: .... Final: ✓....	
Line spacing: 1 .... 2 .... As copy: .✓..	
No of copies required: ....1......	
Paper size: A4 ✓.... A5 .... Portrait: .... Landscape: ✓...	
Date required: ..asap........ Retain on file: ✓.... Delete:	

SPECIAL INSTRUCTIONS:

Please produce a copy of the table attached. Display on either portrait or landscape A4 paper.

ROYAL BIRDWOOD HOTEL, TUNBRIDGE WELLS } (Centre and embolden)

SPECIAL BREAKS

The hotel offers 3 special break prices — the Royale, the Mini and the Golden.

	ROYALE		MINI		GOLDEN*	
	2/1 – 17/5	18/5 – 3/1	2/1 – 17/5	18/5 – 3/1	2/1 – 17/5	18/5 – 3/1
2 nights	100	112	90	98	85	85
Sunday	45	45	36	40	–	–
Extra night	45	50	40	45	45	45
7 nights	295	325	280	290	280	290

ROYALE   Treat yourself to an executive room.

MINI   The rate is per person based on a double or twin-bedded room. Single Supplements apply.

GOLDEN*   This applies to the over 50s and is restricted to a Sunday and Monday night.

All the above rates include accom. for a min. of 2 consecutive nights, full English Breakfast and £16 per person per day towards dinner in the restaurant.

NB. This tariff is subject to alteration without notice.

Check your success

Did you centre and embolden both lines of the heading? ☐

Did you leave consistent spacing between columns? ☐

Did you line up all figures? ☐

Did you expand the abbreviations? ☐

Did you draw the horizontal lines correctly and print on landscape paper? ☐

28   Further editing

Use headers, footers and page numbering
Insert an item extracted from a previous task
Identify and correct inconsistencies of style
Identify and correct 'deliberate' mistakes in both typescript and manuscript
Copy text between pages

You will build on the skills learnt in the earlier sections for editing documents. All the previous skills will be needed and you will be required to demonstrate additional skills.

There will be one document running on to more than one page which will require you to put a **header** and a **footer** on the appropriate pages. Either header or footer could include **page numbering**. There is an automatic command on every system which places the header and footer within the top and bottom margins of the designated pages. You should achieve this by typing the command(s) once and it (they) will then print on each designated page. Some systems show you how the header and footer will print if you go into preview mode.

One task will include dashes or a space where you will be expected to insert the appropriate information having obtained it **from another task**.

As in the Intermediate examination, there will be **deliberate errors**, but these will be spread throughout the tasks and will be in both typescript and manuscript. You will usually be given a hint as to where there are errors within the typescript by the wording on the Word Processing Request Form. There will be no deliberate errors in the stored standard paragraphs. Abbreviations (indicated with full stop) must be expanded.

Throughout the paper you will come across **inconsistencies** in style. For example, these may be a number in figures and then in words, or the time written as the 24-hour clock and then as am and pm.

In the previous stages you have been asked to perform a block move and a block delete. You will now be required to do a **block copy**. This means that the same text must appear in at least 2 places. You should use the block copy facility to do this and not be tempted to retype it. Retyping opens the possibility for errors to creep in.

The following task is taken from a past PEI Examination paper. Please note that in the examination the *recalled task* will have been set up on the candidate's disk by the *tutor*. The first part of this task may therefore be prepared for you by your tutor or you may key in the document yourself.

Note to the Specialist Teacher

Please key in the following text with a minimum left-hand margin of 1" (2.5 cm) and line-spacing as shown.

TASK 3   (Candidate's Name)

(HTOEL) PROSPECTUS

Situated in the beautiful Kent countryside but only a few minutes from the centre of the town, the RBH has built a (sounf) reputation for hospitality and friendliness to match the high (qualtiy) of the service and (accomodation) offered.

The RBH now (baosts) a well-equipped sports and leisure complex in (additoin) to all (it's) other existing facilities.

↑
↓   (leave 3 clear lines)

The friendliness of the RBH and the little bit extra will (be be) obvious immediately on your arrival as you are welcomed by the Hall Porter and the Reception team. Why not relax in the lounge whilst your luggage is taken up to your room.

When you reach (you) room you will find that your luggage is waiting for you. The hotel has 64 bedrooms ranging from 4 (luxurius) suites to single rooms. All rooms (has) private facilities, trouser press, hairdrier, TV, radio, mini bar, tea and coffee-making facilities and telephone.

The hotel offers a range of restaurants to cater for every taste.

The Garden Room is designed to ensure that you can relax and enjoy your choice from the (intresting) menus. Each dish (are) prepared from the freshest food available. This is then cooked to your taste and (attractivly) presented. The accompanying wine list offers a (wideselection) of wines from many countries.

SPECIALIST TEACHER PLEASE NOTE

The above is a proof-reading task. To aid your preparation the "deliberate mistakes" are circled and care should be taken to ensure that errors are repeated when this document is created. Key in with a justified right hand margin.

WORD PROCESSING REQUEST FORM

Task number: .3.	Author's name: m m ....

Create a document: ....   New document name: ....

Edit a document: ..✓.   Existing document name: ....
Datafile: ....   Rename document as: ....

Standard paragraphs are stored as: ....

....

Type of copy: Draft: .✓..   Final: ....

Line spacing: 1 ....   2 .✓..   As copy: ....

No of copies required: .....1....
Paper size: A4 .✓..   A5 ....   Portrait: .✓..   Landscape: ...

Date required: ..a.s.a.p.........   Retain on file: .✓.. Delete: ......

SPECIAL INSTRUCTIONS:

Insert header at top right on every page:
THE HOTEL IN A GARDEN

Insert footer at bottom right on every page:
R___ B___ H___* in full in caps.

change RBH to the full name in all occurrences, but use only initial caps.
This was produced in a hurry please check carefully.
Retain a justified RH margin.

*See page 169.

leave 9 clear line spaces

TASK 3 (Candidate's Name)

HTOEL PROSPECTUS ← underscore

in short walking distance

Situated in the beautiful Kent countryside but ~~only a few minutes~~ from the centre of the town, the RBH has built a sounf reputation for ⋏ hospitality and friendliness to match the high qualtiy of the service and ⋏ accomodation offered.

excellent ⋏

⋏ the standard of

run on copy to **

The RBH now baosts a well-equipped sports and leisure complex ⋏ in additoin to all it's other existing facilities.

⋏ '

leave 1 clear line space only

that extra something

The friendliness of the RBH and ~~the little bit extra~~ ⋏ will be be obvious ~~immediately~~ on your arrival as you are welcomed by the Hall Porter and the Reception team. ~~Why not relax in the lounge whilst your luggage is taken up to your room.~~

NP

NP

uc

will be

When you reach you room ~~you will find that~~ your luggage ~~is~~ waiting for you. The hotel has 64 bedrooms ranging from 4 luxurius suites to single rooms. ⋏ All rooms has private facilities, trouser press, hairdrier, TV, radio, mini bar, tea and coffee-making facilities and telephone.

NP

⋏ Some rooms can be converted into family suites

~~The hotel offers a range of restaurants to cater for every taste.~~ NP

arranged

The Garden Room is ~~designed~~ to ensure that you can relax and enjoy your choice from the intresting menus. Each dish are prepared from the freshest food available. This is then cooked to your taste and attractivly presented. The accompanying wine list offers a wideselection of wines from many countries.

stet move to *

RESTAURANTS

leave 2" (5cm) by 1" (2.5cm) for a symbol

The hotel has a variety of restaurants in which you can eat. These are organised so th. you can choose the style of menu and the type of surroundings to suite your mood. The choices are between the Garden Rm., the Table Basket Rm., the Terrace Bar and the Grill Rm. There shd. be something to suit all tastes.

for a relaxed atmosphere try the Grill Rm.
overlooking the swimming pool. You choose from
a selection of meat or fish + these are then
charcoal - grilled to taste and served with
vegs. or a fresh salad. You can also choose
a light snack from the extensive menu.

A lighter meal is available at the Table Basket
Rm. where a wide range of beers is also
served.
*
To complete your choice a salad buffet is
avail. every day between 11.30 am + 14 30
hours in the Terrace Bar + a roast lunch is
served on a Sun. in the Garden Room.

* *
The heated swimming pool is surrounded
by tropical flowers + palm trees. A children's
pool, jacuzzi and a sauna are also
available. If you are feeling energetic,
you can have a game of squash in the
glass - walled courts or work out in the
gymnasium under qualified supervision.

Check your success   Did you successfully run your headers and footers?   ☐

Did you change 'RBH' to 'Royal Birdwood Hotel' in all instances?   ☐

Did you put the full document into double line spacing?   ☐

Did you follow all the editing instructions?   ☐

Did you *copy* the paragraph beginning 'The RBH now boasts...' to appear   ☐
again as the penultimate paragraph?

Did you leave an accurate space of 2" (5 cm) by 1" (2.5 cm)?   ☐

Did you expand all abbreviations and correct all 'deliberate' mistakes?   ☐

Did you notice the inconsistency in the times (11.30 am and 1430 hours) and alter   ☐
one of them?

The following task is taken from a past PEI Examination paper. Please note that in the examination the *recalled task* will have been set up on the candidate's disk by the *tutor*. The first part of this task may therefore be prepared for you by your tutor or you may key in the document yourself.

Note to Specialist Teacher

The following paragraphs need to be keyed in so that candidates can recall them to produce standard letters. If your system has a library document facility then they can be typed into this. If no such facility exists, please key them into separate files.

Please key in either with <u>enter</u> points or by inserting code symbols eg & or @ to indicate the enter points.

TASK 4   (Candidate's Name)

PARAGRAPH 1

Fees for the Royal Birdwood Hotel Leisure Complex apply for the forthcoming year - January to January. Prices are calculated per month on the remaining months or parts of month.

PARAGRAPH 2

FULL MEMBERSHIP

Single membership @
Couple membership @
Family membership @

PARAGRAPH 3

Gold Card membership @
Silver Card membership @

PARAGRAPH 4

SUNBED USERS' FEES

Members (20 minutes) @
Non-members (20 minutes) @
Members (6 sessions) @
Non-members (6 sessions) @

PARAGRAPH 5

Your first introductory familiarisation session can be free of charge - telephone 776329 to book your free session.

WORD PROCESSING REQUEST FORM

Task number: .4.	Author's name: ...MM.... (Margaret Mason) General Manager

Create a document: .✓.. New document name: ....

Edit a document: .... Existing document name: ....

Datafile: .... Rename document as: ....

Standard paragraphs are stored as: ....

....

Type of copy: Draft: ....   Final: .✓..

Line spacing: 1 ....   2 ....   As copy: .✓..

No of copies required: ../.......

Paper size: A4 ✓..   A5 ....   Portrait: .✓..   Landscape: ...

Date required: .today........   Retain on file: ✓.. Delete: ......

SPECIAL INSTRUCTIONS:

Please send the attached letter & use the standard paras already stored.
You will need the following info:
Single mbr. £80.00; Couple £150;
Family £166.50
Gold card - £100; Silver £75.00

NB. The copy of standard paras is for reference only.

Mr N Allwood
16 The Bridges
SOUTH BOROUGH
TN3 6NX

Dear Mr _____

NP Thank you for your letter of last Friday [I am sorry to hear that your stay with us was less than perfect. I regret that you did not contact me whilst you were at the hotel as I am sure we could have satisfactorily resolved the problems of the plumbing in your room. [Please accept the 2 enclosed complimentary vouchers for a meal for two in our restaurant.]

I am pleased that you wish to consider joining our Leisure Complex membership scheme.

Paras 1, 2, 3, 5 here please (double line space para 5 & inset 1" (2·5cm) from both margins).

indent this as a new para - 1" (2·5 cm) from left margin

Yours sincerely

M _____ M _____

Check your success

Did you produce one letter and did you remember to date it? ☐

Did you remember to indicate the enclosure? ☐

Did you insert the correct paragraphs? ☐

Did you remember to change paragraph 5 to double line spacing and indent it 1″ (2.5 cm) from both margins? ☐

Did you indent the correct paragraph from the left margin? ☐

Did you notice the inconsistency in numbers (2 and two) and make them both the same? ☐

Did you insert the correct names at the dashes? ☐

29 Mail merge

Create a standard document
Merge it with specified records or an existing datafile

Mail merge (or list processing) is the automatic facility by which you can merge a standard document (eg a letter) with a datafile (eg a list of names and addresses) so that several documents are produced, each with individual information in them. The information which is different for each document produced is called a **variable**.

To run a mail merge you need to produce at least 2 documents:

1 the **datafile** containing the list of variable information to be inserted into the master document
2 the **master document** (often a letter or invoice) containing points where information is to be inserted from the datafile.

You then need to give the computer instructions as to which datafile to merge with which standard document. These instructions may be on the standard document or separate, depending on your system.

In the Advanced Word Processing examination, your tutor will prepare a datafile containing 4 records. You will be asked to create a standard document and to merge it with all the records in the datafile. In order to do this you must first of all view the datafile to see how your tutor has keyed it in. Note what type of information is in each record so that you know what variables to put in your standard document. You may find it useful to jot down quickly details of the first record. At this level of examination each record will be of the same length.

You must then key in the standard document, making any necessary amendments, and putting merge codes at the points where you need to pick up the information from the datafile. Do not forget to put a page break at the end of the document so that, when you run the mail merge, the 4 documents are printed on separate pieces of paper.

You may find it useful to run the mail merge and store it on disk rather than run it straight through the printer. You can then view the results on screen to check that they are correct and that the correct variables have been inserted into the correct spaces before you print. If you find mistakes, return to your standard document, make corrections and run the mail merge again. When this is correct, print it out.

Example

Datafile

Ms P O'Boyle	Mr J Patel	Mrs L Mi	Mr R Rowe
Park House	12 Main Street	18 Peacock Way	Highlands
High Street	Yadavagiri	Lowlands	Park View
Auckland	Mysore	Scarborough	Glasgow
New Zealand	India	Tobago	Scotland
Ms Boyle	Mr Patel	Mrs Mi	Mr Rowe
Singapore	Delhi	Miami	Paris

Standard Letter

Ref PM/aa

(Today's date)

&name&
&address1&
&address2&
&address3&
&country&

Dear &salutation&

Thank you for your recent enquiry for information on the
International Conference at &place&. I am pleased to enclose
further details and a booking form.

Yours sincerely

P Matthew
Conference Organiser

encs

Obviously you will need to set these up according to your system and only a guideline
can be covered here.

Create a datafile with the following information so that it will merge with a standard letter.

Mr P Martin	Ms D Turner	Mr P Shah	Mr T Amoh
23 Crossways	Flat 456	23 Kenyatta Road	Taylors Way
Fairways	Napier Street	Newlands	Western Road
Wellington	Kowloon	Nairobi	Kingston
New Zealand	Hong Kong	Kenya	Jamaica
3	12	4	6

Key in the following standard letter and merge it with the datafile already created. Print one copy of each letter with a justified right margin please.

Ref MR/(your initials)

*

Dear *

Thank you for yr. enquiry regarding tickets for the International Symposium to be held this year in Geneva. As you will know, tickets are allocated by ballot. You have been allocated * tickets.

(insert the date of the last Friday in the month)

Please let me know by Friday ↵ if you wish to take up some or all of this allocation. If we do not hear from you, your tickets will be placed in the draw again & allocated to others.

I hope you will attend the Symposium. Further details will be sent to you in 2 months' time.

Yrs sincerely

Michael Royston
Organiser

Practice from the paper

The following task is taken from a past PEI Examination paper. Please note that in the examination the *recalled task* will have been set up on the candidate's disk by the *tutor*. The first part of this task may therefore be prepared for you by your tutor or you may key in the document yourself. See pages 169 and 178 for other information required.

This task tests the following competences:

Checklist reference 29   mail merge
Checklist reference 28   inserting item extracted from a previous task
Checklist reference 21.2   expand abbreviations
Checklist reference 22   justification

Note to Specialist Teacher

Please create a datafile and key in the following addresses for candidates to merge with a prepared standard letter.

TASK 2   (Candidate's Name)

Mr and Mrs T Turner
123 Brian's Wood
LEEDS
LS2 8TG
Mr and Mrs Turner
12 July

Mr and Mrs B Ali
Hunterton
SHEFFIELD
S34 6NG
Mr and Mrs Ali
26 July

Mr and Mrs Y Shah
Jardinere Grove
SKIPTON
Y45 2BT
Mr and Mrs Shah
3 August

Mr and Mrs P Greene
Kingsmede
LINCOLN
LN2 1TH
Mr and Mrs Greene
10 August

WORD PROCESSING REQUEST FORM

Task number: .2.   Author's name: ...MM....................................

Create A documents ..✓.. New document name: ....

Edit a document: ....   Existing document name: ....

Datafile: ....   Rename document as: ....

Standard paragraphs are stored as: ....

. . . .

Type of copy: Draft: ....   Final: ✓...

Line spacing: 1 ✓...   2 ....   As copy: ....

No of copies required: .1 of each

Paper size: A4 ✓..   A5 ....   Portrait: .✓.   Landscape: ...

Date required: .today......   Retain on file: .✓.. Delete: ......

SPECIAL INSTRUCTIONS:

Please examine the datafile then
key in the attached standard
letter. Merge it with the datafile
already created & print 1 copy
of each letter.

Justify right margin please.

TASK 2 (Candidate's Name)

Dear

Please kind + insert

Thank you for returning the completed booking form.

I confirm th. I am pleased to be able to offer you accom. in the hotel for 7 days from * for 2 persons. This will be on our Royale Break + the rate per person will be ↗

Each executive room contains en suite facilities, hairdrier, trouser press, tea + coffee-making facilities, TV, radio, mini bar + telephone. There is a complimentary basket of fruit in each room on arrival.

The hotel offers a full range of menus - both à la carte + table d'hôte. Vegetarian menus are always available.

I am enclosing a copy of our brochure + if there is anything you wish to confirm before your arrival, please do not hesitate to contact me.

Yours sincerely
R ___ B ___ H ___

M ___ M ___
G ___ M ___

Check your success

Did you remember to date the letter? □

Did you produce 4 letters? □

Were all the variables correctly entered? □

Did each letter print out on a separate sheet of paper? □

Did you remember to justify the right margin? □

Did you find and insert all the information required? □

Did you expand all abbreviations? □

Did you type 'coffee-making' with a hyphen and 'menus — both à la carte' with a dash? □

Did you remember to indicate the enclosure? □

30   Advanced examination questions

There now follows an Advanced examination paper, which has been worked through and solutions provided.

If you wish, you may work through the paper yourself before comparing your printouts with the solutions provided.

In order to 'mirror' examination conditions, it will be necessary for your *Specialist Teacher* to set up those tasks which need to be stored on disk prior to the commencement of the examination paper.

Further practice   For further practice, copies of past papers can be obtained from PEI. It is suggested that you practise on as many past papers as you can before taking the examination.
Note: For further helpful hints, *see* **Section 35 Preparing for the Word Processing examinations**.

```
┌─────────────────────────────────────┐
│                                      │
│   WORD PROCESSING - ADVANCED         │
│                                      │
│                                      │
└─────────────────────────────────────┘
```

PITMAN
EXAMINATIONS
INSTITUTE

No.

To be handed to Specialist Teacher before the date of the examination

This pack contains:

> One Specialist Teacher's Instructions
> and details of Tasks to be created on storage medium.

1   In advance of the date of the examination, you are asked to create documents on the storage medium for the attached tasks.

2   You may key in text using character line length for any appropriate pitch.

3   With the exception of line endings, which may vary with the choice of pitch, please follow the text <u>exactly</u> (including "deliberate mistakes").

4   Copies of these documents should be created on the storage medium for the exclusive use of each individual candidate.

5   <u>Print out a copy of your work to be attached to the Attestation Form for the examination.</u>

6   Because word processing systems vary so widely between Centres it is not possible for the Examiner to specify file names for documents. Please allocate suitable file names for the documents created (TASK 1, TASK 2, etc are suggested, as appropriate). Likewise, please devise suitable file names for candidates to store their completed tasks.

7   Please complete the spaces provided on each of the WORD PROCESSING REQUEST FORMS, or as otherwise indicated, so that these file names will be available to candidates at the start of the examination.

8   The preparation of all examination material must be regarded as strictly confidential and should be carried out under the supervision of the Invigilator. No details of the content of the examination may be divulged, and the Specialist Teacher and Invigilator are asked to sign the Attestation Form to this effect. This should be enclosed with the worked scripts, together with a printed specimen copy of each of the prepared tasks.

9   All material must be erased from the system and storage medium at the end of the examination after the completion of all the required printing.

1991

Please create a datafile and key in the following addresses for candidates to merge with a prepared standard letter.

TASK 2   (Candidate's Name)

Mr H Bradbury
2 Trenance Gardens
KEIGHLEY
West Yorkshire
United Kingdom
Mr Bradbury
INTRODUCTION TO ART - P56

Miss L Johns
9 Bolton Road
Halbeath
DUNFERMLINE
Scotland
Miss Johns
PASTELS - P23

Mr H Baig
19 Lake Placid Bay
CALGARY
Alberta
Canada
Mr Baig
SKETCHING - A21

Mrs K Chang
234 Jalan Sultan
KUALA LUMPUR
Malaysia
Mrs Chang
WATER COLOURS - P39

TASK 3   (Candidate's Name)

INTRODUCTION TO ART - COURSE NUMBER P56

Materials and Equipment

You will now need to equip yourself with a few basic requirements in order to take Number P56 Course. These are listed below:

PENCILS

You will reuqire HB, B and 3B pencils of any good make. The letters indicate the degree of softness of the lead. HB, meaning hard black, is a medium grade and prodcues a fairly fine grey line when sharpned. The grades then are labelled in numerical order, B, 2B, 3B etc. 6B is a verysoft grade. At the other end of the scale are the H grades. These are too hard for most sketching exercises.

The HB pencil id suitable for most general work while the softer pencils are more suit able for tonal drawing since they give a softer, blacker mark.

ERASER
A good soft india-rubber eraser or putty rubber is needed but you must try to restrict the amount of rubbing out to the mininum. Some teachers suggests that students throw thier rubber away in the early stages of learning!

PAPER

For Number P56 Course you shuold purchace white imperial cartridge paper, half imperial size along with a pocket-size sketch pad.

DRAWING BOARD

A spruce drawing board is the ideel surface to draw on but any piece of flat board is suitable providing that the surfcae is smooth.

GOUACHE COLOURS

For Number P56 Course you will needs to purchase a minimum of colours-Spectrum Yellow, Spectrum Red, Periwinkle Blue, Ivory Black and Permanent White.

These are a type of water colour since water is used to dilute them. However, unlike water colours these are opaque and do not rely on the white paper underneath them to give a degree of lightness. Lightness is obtained by adding more white gouache.

SPECIALIST TEACHER PLEASE NOTE

The above is a proof-reading task. To aid your preparation the "deliberate mistakes" are circled and care should be taken to ensure that errors are repeated when this document is created.

_____

<u>TASK 4</u>   (Candidate's Name)

<u>STANDARD PARAGRAPH 1</u>

INTRODUCTION TO ART

The Workshop to support this course is organised by @. It will take place from 3-5 July.

<u>STANDARD PARAGRAPH 2</u>

SKETCHING

A one-day seminar will be held on 19 August by the tutor on this course, @.

<u>STANDARD PARAGRAPH 3</u>

PASTELS

A week-end activity course will take place in the Lake District on 24-25 October in order to catch the beautiful autumn tints. The tutors for this are @ and @.

<u>STANDARD PARAGRAPH 4</u>

OIL PAINTING

A week's course has been arranged from 14 September to examine techniques used by 6 modern oil painters. The course organiser is @.

<u>STANDARD PARAGRAPH 5</u>

ACRYLICS

The use of these paints is covered in a one-day activity session led by the famous artist, Rena Baghara and the course tutor, @.

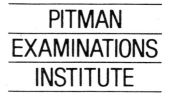

No.

CANDIDATE'S NAME ....
(Block letters please)

CENTRE NO. ....DATE ....

This examination lasts for 2 hours and consists of four tasks which you should file on the storage medium for printing out later. The Invigilator will give you instructions about arrangements for printing out your documents.

You have 10 minutes to read through the tasks and documents before starting the examination. Check that you have been given all the document names required to create, recall or store your finished work.

FOR EXAMINER'S USE ONLY

COMPLETION	ACCURACY	DISPLAY

© Sir Isaac Pitman Ltd   1991

INSTRUCTIONS TO CANDIDATES

You work as a word processor operator for Robert Westwood,
Customer Liaison Manager of Homebase - a Correspondence
College specialising in tutorial courses on art. Each day your
in-tray contains a mixture of new tasks and amended
documents returned by their authors.

Carry out the tasks attached, following any instructions given
on the Word Processing Request Forms or on the documents
themselves. Take care to proof-read and correct any errors.

You may carry out the tasks in any order you think appropriate.
However, please collate the printouts in the correct sequence.

WORD PROCESSING REQUEST FORM

Task number: ..1....... Author's name: .RW.....................

Create a document: .✓... New document name: ....

Edit a document: .... Existing document name: ....

Rename document as: ....

Standard paragraphs are stored as:

....

....

....

Type of copy: Draft: .... Final: .✓...............

Line spacing: 1 .... 2 .... As copy: .✓...........

No of copies required: ..1................................

Paper size: A4 .✓... A5 ..... Portrait: ..... Landscape: .✓...*

Date required: ..asap.... Retain on file: .✓.. Delete: ....

SPECIAL INSTRUCTIONS:

Please produce a copy of the Information Leaflet attached.

* Landscape preferred, but if not use A4 portrait.

HOMEBASE

CORRESPONDENCE COURSES IN ART ⟩ centre + embolden

The following courses are available:

Course No	Title	Level	Tutor	Course Fees	
				Full Tuition	No Tuition
P 56	Introduction to Art	Beginner	Roy Long	104	84
A 21	Sketching	Beginner	Mary Parker	104	—
P 39	Water colours	Beginner	Rhihini Bi	104	—
P 23	Pastels	Beginner	John Cheung	104	—
R 74	Oil Painting	Beginner	Mark Changa	104	—
B 51	Acrylics	Beginner	Sally Wood	104	—
P 40	Water Colouring	Advanced	Graham Peters	156	—
P 24	Advanced Pastels	Advanced	Raymond Good	156	—
R 75	Advanced Oil Painting	Advanced	kitu Chandra	156	—

Prices include postage (airmail for overseas) and are subject to alteration without notice. You may pay yr. fee in full by cheque, postal order or banker's draft. This wl. save you paying the Instalment Fee. Alternatively you may pay by instalments. Add £12 to the fee, divide by 3, send a third with your enrolement and then 2 equal monthly instalments.

WORD PROCESSING REQUEST FORM

Task number: ..2...... Author's name: .RW.....................

Create a document:^s .✓... New document name: ....

Edit a document: .... Existing document name: ....

Rename document as: ....

Standard paragraphs are stored as:

....

....

....

Type of copy: Draft: .... Final: ..✓..............

Line spacing: 1 ..✓........ 2 .... As copy: ....

No of copies required: ./.of.each...........................

Paper size: A4 .✓... A5 ..... Portrait: .✓... Landscape: .....

Date required: .today.... Retain on file: .✓... Delete: ....

SPECIAL INSTRUCTIONS:

Please examine the datafile then key in the attached standard letter. Merge it with the datafile already created + print 1 copy of each letter.

Justify the right margin please.

Please complete the letter as usual with the Company name, my name + job title.

Dear

RE : COURSE @

Thank you for your application form and cheque for the above course. I am pleased to welcome you as a student of the College + to send you your course materials tog. with :

Indent
½"
½
(1.5cm)
from
left.
margin

1   the name and address of your tutor

2   ten prepared labels to be used when sending yr. work to yr. tutor

3   a record of work form for you to complete (the top copy of this must be sent to your tutor with your 1st assignment + the second copy is for you to keep a record of your progress on the course)

4   an envelope to be used when you send your work to your tutor.

Tuition is for a period of 2 yrs. You can work at your own pace + send in work to your tutor when you are ready. However it is recommended that regular study produces max. benefit.

Remember to quote your College reg. no. on all your work.

If you meet any difficulties with your course, please do not hesitate to contact me. I hope th. you will enjoy the course + derive much benefit from it.

Yours sincerely

WORD PROCESSING REQUEST FORM

Task number: ..3...... Author's name: ..RW...................

Create a document: ..... New document name: ....

Edit a document: ..✓.... Existing document name: ....

Rename document as: ....

Standard paragraphs are stored as:

....

....

....

Type of copy: Draft: ....✓............ Final: ....

Line spacing: 1 .... 2 .... As copy: ...✓........

No of copies required: .1.......................................

Paper size: A4 .✓... A5 ..... Portrait: .✓... Landscape: .....

Date required: asap...... Retain on file: .✓.. Delete: ....

SPECIAL INSTRUCTIONS:

Insert header at top right of each page:
INTRODUCTION TO ART
Insert footer at bottom right of every page:
PS6/RW/932
Replace: Number PS6 with Introduction to Art.
Do this in all occurrences but the main heading.

This was produced in a hurry, please check
carefully.
Paginate sensibly.

TASK 3   *[copy to end of page 2]*   (Candidate's name)

INTRODUCTION TO ART - COURSE NUMBER P56 ← *underscore*

[leave 6 clear lines] Materials and Equipment ← *change to caps*

You will now need to equip yourself with a few basic requirements in order to take Number P56 Course. These are listed below:

PENCILS   ∧ *These will be useful time and time again.*

∧ You will reuqire HB, B and 3B pencils of any ~~good~~ *reputable* make. The letters indicate the degree of softness of the lead. HB, meaning hard black, is a medium grade and prodcues a fairly fine grey line when sharpned. The grades then are labelled in numerical order, B, 2B, 3B etc. 6B is a very soft grade. At the other end of the scale are the H grades. ~~These are too hard for most sketching exercises.~~ *stet*

run on The HB pencil id suitable for most ~~general~~ *ordinary* work while the softer pencils are more *trs* suit able for tonal drawing since they give a (softer) (blacker) mark.

ERASER   *insert line space*

erasing A good soft india-rubber eraser or putty rubber is needed but you must try to restrict the amount of ~~rubbing out~~ to the mininum. Some teachers suggests that students throw thier rubber away in the early stages of learning!

PAPER   *a good supply of*

✱ insert Ⓐ here For Number P56 Course you shuold purchace white imperial cartridge paper, half imperial size along with a *thick* pocket-size sketch pad

DRAWING BOARD

1 line space only *on which to rest your paper*

A spruce drawing board is the ideel surface ~~to draw on~~ but any piece of flat board is suitable providing that the surfcae is smooth.

move to Ⓑ GOUACHE COLOURS

For Number P56 Course you will needs to purchase a minimum of colours-Spectrum Yellow, Spectrum Red, Periwinkle Blue, Ivory Black and Permanent White.   , ∧

These are a type of water colour since water is used to dilute them. However, unlike water colours these are opaque and do not rely on the white paper underneath them to give a degree of lightness. Lightness is obtained by adding more white gouache.

(A) A set of 4 drawing board clips is the best way to hold your paper firmly. However, large brass drawing pins could be used instead.

DRAWING PENS

A selection of pens is needed. These include a mapping pen for the finest line work + a range of nibs for drawing lines of diff. thicknesses.

CONTE CRAYONS

These should be on hand but should not be used until you have experience of using the pencil. They are about 7 centimetres in length and are square in section. They produce a soft black chalky line or can be used to produce large areas of flat tone.

(B) →

Water Colours

A 12-pan box of student quality should be sufficient to begin with.

double line spacing + indent 1" (2.5 cm) from both margins.

This equipment is sufficient for most artists + can always be added to as you become more proficient.

Task number: ..4...... Author's name: ..RW.........................

Create a document: ..✓.... New document name: ....

Edit a document: .... Existing document name: ....
Rename document as: ....
Standard paragraphs are stored as:
..①.............................②...............................
..③.............................④...............................
..⑤...

Type of copy: Draft: .... Final: ..✓...............

Line spacing: 1 .... 2 .... As copy: ..✓..........

No of copies required: ../.................................
Paper size: A4 .✓... A5 ..... Portrait: ✓.... Landscape: .....

Date required: ..today... Retain on file: ✓... Delete: ....

SPECIAL INSTRUCTIONS:

Please send the attached letter and use the
standard paras. already stored. You will need
the following information:
the tutors for the courses are those in
the information leaflet with the addition
of Robin Cammish who assists on the
Pastels Course.

NB. The copy of the std. paras. is for reference
only.

Mrs M Raghani
PO Box 9137
RUWI
Sultanate of Oman

Dear _____

Thank you for your letter of (insert date of last Thurs).

I am pleased that you are enjoying your course on Introduction to Art. We always enjoy receiving letters from our students & use the comments when we are reviewing our course materials - something that we do all *NP* the time. [You ask for details of other related art courses. I am sending full details of these & am enclosing details of forthcoming events that may be of interest to you.

(Insert paras 1, 3, 4, 5 here)

I look forward to hearing from you.

Yours sincerely
H ____

R _____ W ____
C _____ L _____ M _____

TASK 4   (Candidate's name)

STANDARD PARAGRAPH 1

INTRODUCTION TO ART

The Workshop to support this course is organised by @. It will take place from 3-5 July.

STANDARD PARAGRAPH 2

SKETCHING

A one-day seminar will be held on 19 August by the tutor on this course, @.

STANDARD PARAGRAPH 3

PASTELS

A week-end activity course will take place in the Lake District on 24-25 October in order to catch the beautiful autumn tints. The tutors for this are @ and @.

STANDARD PARAGRAPH 4

OIL PAINTING

A week's course has been arranged from 14 September to examine techniques used by 6 modern oil painters. The course organiser is @.

STANDARD PARAGRAPH 5

ACRYLICS

The use of these paints is covered in a one-day activity session led by the famous artist, Rena Baghara and the course tutor, @.

TASK 1

(Candidate's name)

HOMEBASE

CORRESPONDENCE COURSES IN ART

The following courses are available:

Course No	Title	Level	Tutor	Course Fees	
				Full Tuition	No Tuition
P56	Introduction to Art	Beginner	Roy Lang	104	84
A21	Sketching	Beginner	Mary Parker	104	-
P39	Water Colours	Beginner	Rhahini Bi	104	-
P23	Pastels	Beginner	John Cheung	104	-
R74	Oil Painting	Beginner	Mark Changa	104	-
B51	Acrylics	Beginner	Sally Wood	104	-
P40	Water Colouring	Advanced	Graham Peters	156	-
P24	Advanced Pastels	Advanced	Raymond Good	156	-
R75	Advanced Oil Painting	Advanced	Kitu Chandra	156	-

Prices include postage (airmail for overseas) and are subject to alteration without notice. You may pay your fee in full by cheque, postal order or banker's draft. This will save you paying the Instalment Fee. Alternatively you may pay by instalments. Add £12 to the fee, divide by 3, send a third with your enrolment and then 2 equal monthly instalments.

19 October 1992

Mr H Bradbury
2 Trenance Gardens
KEIGHLEY
West Yorkshire
United Kingdom

Dear Mr Bradbury

RE: COURSE INTRODUCTION TO ART - P56

Thank you for your application form and cheque for the above course. I am pleased to welcome you as a student of the College and to send you your course materials together with:

1   the name and address of your tutor

2   10 prepared labels to be used when sending your work to your tutor

3   a record of work form for you to complete (the top copy of this must be sent to your tutor with your first assignment and the second copy is for you to keep a record of your progress on the course)

4   an envelope to be used when you send your work to your tutor.

Tuition is for a period of 2 years. You can work at your own pace and send in work to your tutor when you are ready. However it is recommended that regular study produces maximum benefit.

Remember to quote your College registration number on all your work.

If you meet any difficulties with your course, please do not hesitate to contact me. I hope that you will enjoy the course and derive much benefit from it.

Yours sincerely
HOMEBASE

ROBERT WESTWOOD
Customer Liaison Manager

encs

TASK 2   (Candidate's name)

19 October 1992

Miss L Johns
9 Bolton Road
Halbeath
DUNFERMLINE
Scotland

Dear Miss Johns

RE: COURSE PASTELS - P23

Thank you for your application form and cheque for the above
course. I am pleased to welcome you as a student of the College
and to send you your course materials together with:

    1   the name and address of your tutor

    2   10 prepared labels to be used when sending your work to
        your tutor

    3   a record of work form for you to complete (the top copy of
        this must be sent to your tutor with your first assignment
        and the second copy is for you to keep a record of your
        progress on the course)

    4   an envelope to be used when you send your work to your
        tutor.

Tuition is for a period of 2 years. You can work at your own
pace and send in work to your tutor when you are ready. However
it is recommended that regular study produces maximum benefit.

Remember to quote your College registration number on all your
work.

If you meet any difficulties with your course, please do not
hesitate to contact me. I hope that you will enjoy the course
and derive much benefit from it.

Yours sincerely
HOMEBASE

ROBERT WESTWOOD
Customer Liaison Manager

encs

19 October 1992

Mr H Baig
19 Lake Placid Bay
CALGARY
Alberta
Canada

Dear Mr Baig

RE: COURSE SKETCHING - A21

Thank you for your application form and cheque for the above course. I am pleased to welcome you as a student of the College and to send you your course materials together with:

1 the name and address of your tutor

2 10 prepared labels to be used when sending your work to your tutor

3 a record of work form for you to complete (the top copy of this must be sent to your tutor with your first assignment and the second copy is for you to keep a record of your progress on the course)

4 an envelope to be used when you send your work to your tutor.

Tuition is for a period of 2 years. You can work at your own pace and send in work to your tutor when you are ready. However it is recommended that regular study produces maximum benefit.

Remember to quote your College registration number on all your work.

If you meet any difficulties with your course, please do not hesitate to contact me. I hope that you will enjoy the course and derive much benefit from it.

Yours sincerely
HOMEBASE

ROBERT WESTWOOD
Customer Liaison Manager

encs

19 October 1992

Mrs K Chang
234 Jalan Sultan
KUALA LUMPUR
Malaysia

Dear Mrs Chang

RE: COURSE WATER COLOURS - P39

Thank you for your application form and cheque for the above
course. I am pleased to welcome you as a student of the College
and to send you your course materials together with:

    1   the name and address of your tutor

    2   10 prepared labels to be used when sending your work to
        your tutor

    3   a record of work form for you to complete (the top copy of
        this must be sent to your tutor with your first assignment
        and the second copy is for you to keep a record of your
        progress on the course)

    4   an envelope to be used when you send your work to your
        tutor.

Tuition is for a period of 2 years. You can work at your own
pace and send in work to your tutor when you are ready. However
it is recommended that regular study produces maximum benefit.

Remember to quote your College registration number on all your
work.

If you meet any difficulties with your course, please do not
hesitate to contact me. I hope that you will enjoy the course
and derive much benefit from it.

Yours sincerely
HOMEBASE

ROBERT WESTWOOD
Customer Liaison Manager

encs

TASK 3   (Candidate's Name)

INTRODUCTION TO ART - COURSE NUMBER P56

MATERIALS AND EQUIPMENT

You will now need to equip yourself with a few basic requirements
in order to take Introduction to Art Course. These will be
useful time and time again. These are listed below:

PENCILS

You will require HB, B and 3B pencils of any reputable make. The
letters indicate the degree of softness of the lead. HB, meaning
hard black, is a medium grade and produces a fairly fine grey
line when sharpened. The grades then are labelled in numerical
order, B, 2B, 3B etc. 6B is a very soft grade. At the other end
of the scale are the H grades. The HB pencil is suitable for
most general work while the softer pencils are more suitable for
tonal drawing since they give a blacker, softer mark.

ERASER

A good soft india-rubber eraser or putty rubber is needed but you
must try to restrict the amount of erasing to the minimum.
Some teachers suggest that students throw their rubber away in
the early stages of learning!

PAPER

For Introduction to Art Course you should purchase a good supply
of white imperial cartridge paper, half imperial size along with
a thick pocket-size sketch pad.

A set of 4 drawing board clips is the bestway to hold your paper
firmly. However, large brass drawing pins could be used instead.

DRAWING BOARD

A spruce drawing board is the ideal surface on which to rest your
paper but any piece of board is suitable providing that the
surface is smooth.

DRAWING PENS

A selection of pens is needed. These include a mapping pen for
the finest line work and a range of nibs for drawing lines of
different thicknesses.

P56/RW/932

CONTE CRAYONS

These should be on hand but should not be used until you have experience of using the pencil. They are about 7 centimetres in length and are square in section. They produce a soft black chalky line or can be used to produce large areas of flat tone.

GOUACHE COLOURS

For Introduction to Art Course you will need to purchase a minimum of colours - Spectrum Yellow, Spectrum Red, Periwinkle Blue, Ivory, Black and Permanent White.

WATER COLOURS

A 12-pan box of student quality should be sufficient to begin with.

This equipment is sufficient for most artists

and can always be added to as you become more

proficient.

INTRODUCTION TO ART - COURSE NUMBER P56

P56/RW/932

19 October 1992

Mrs M Raghani
PO Box 9137
RUWI
Sultanate of Oman

Dear Mrs Raghani

Thank you for your letter of 15 October 1992.

I am pleased that you are enjoying your course on Introduction to
Art. We always enjoy receiving letters from our students and use
the comments when we are reviewing our course materials -
something that we do all the time.

You ask for details of other related art courses. I am sending you
full details of these and am enclosing details of forthcoming
events that may be of interest to you.

INTRODUCTION TO ART

The Workshop to support this course is organised by Roy Lang. It
will take place from 3-5 July.

PASTELS

A week-end activity course will take place in the Lake District
on 24-25 October in order to catch the beautiful autumn tints.
The tutors for this are John Cheung and Robin Cammish.

OIL PAINTING

A week's course has been arranged from 14 September to examine
techniques used by 6 modern oil painters. The course organiser
is Mark Changa.

ACRYLICS

The use of these paints is covered in a one-day activity session
led by the famous artist, Rena Baghara and the course tutor,
Sally Wood.

I look forward to hearing from you.

Yours sincerely
HOMEBASE

Robert Westwood
CUSTOMER LIAISON MANAGER

encs

Part 4 **Masterclass**

Instructions for Part 4

If you have already acquired word processing skills at advanced level, either by completing the first three parts of this guide or through practical experience in the workplace, then you will find the following break-down of the competences required to be successful in the **Masterclass Word Processing** examination appropriate to your needs.

The same approach as in Parts 1, 2 and 3 has been adopted whereby a skill is firstly *identified*, then *practised* using example material and material from a past PEI examination paper, and then assessed. The areas of knowledge and skills to be achieved follow the sequence set out in the **checklist**.

You are advised to maintain a **portfolio** of your work with a copy of the **checklist** for recording your progress.

Syllabus

Word Processing — Masterclass

(Time allowed — 2 hours excluding printing time, plus 10 minutes reading time.)

Aim

The aim of the examination is to examine word processing operating skills at a Masterclass level in terms of accuracy, layout and presentation, and production rate.

Target population

The examination is designed for candidates who want certification of superior level operating skills using word processing software. It is intended for those who have already achieved advanced level qualifications and now aspire to a higher level qualification which tests the ability to use a range of facilities. The examination would, therefore, be suitable for supervisory or senior secretarial staff who wish to obtain recognition for their complete mastery of word processing, or for secretarial and business studies students who have already achieved advanced level proficiency.

Candidates should have a good command of English, numerical skills and knowledge of current business practice and be able to carry out non-routine tasks without supervision.

Objectives

To complete the examination, the candidate should be able to:

1. Organise work tasks and storage and printing resources in an appropriate manner for efficient word processing by:

    - switching on the hardware/logging on to system
    - inserting software and work disks where necessary
    - loading program to memory
    - formatting blank disks
    - extracting work details from job sheets
    - selecting appropriate stationery
    - using appropriate pitch
    - using spellcheck facility
    - backing-up work disks
    - closing down the system/logging off the system.

2. Set up suitable formats for creating new documents by resetting default values as required and including margins, line spacing, page size, tabs.

3. Key in from hard copy, and file. Hard copy will include amended manuscript and typescript, text and figures including subscripts and superscripts and composite characters, leader dots, indented texts and columns.

4. Retrieve stored documents; assemble documents from standard paragraphs; insert variable information in standard documents.

5. Select information from one document for inclusion within another.

6. Edit documents by moving and copying within and between pages, insertion and deletion, search and replace, highlighting and centring.

7. Proof-read and correct on screen as necessary.

8 Amend layout, spacing and presentation of documents by margin changes, line spacing alterations, right margin justification, repagination, and automatic re-numbering of paragraphs.

9 Create a standard document and a datafile.

10 Merge and print using all or selected items from the datafile.

11 Create and revise multi-column and tabular (including decimal) formats.

12 Sort a list of items into either ascending or descending, alphabetical or numerical order.

13 Use headers, footers, page numbering and footnoting facilities.

14 Use contents and indexing facilities.

15 Use maths facilities to add, subtract, multiply and divide.

16 Use line drawing facilities to produce simple charts and tables.

17 Prepare a selection of documents from the following:

Business letter
Memorandum
Report
Form or form letter
Agenda
Minutes
Legal document
Circular
Balance Sheet.

18 Print documents in required styles by using single sheet, landscape and portrait, headed and continuous stationery, changing ribbons and printwheels.

The examination

The examination will consist of 4 in-tray assignments and the candidate will be assumed to be working in one organisation. Each examination will contain both (a) text to be created and stored, and (b) text to be retrieved for revision. The candidate will be judged on the quality of the printed output he or she produces.
   Note: **Masterclass only – candidates are *not* permitted to print documents during the examination for reference purposes**.

Assessment

Candidates' performance will be assessed on the criteria of accuracy, presentation and production rate.
   To achieve a **Pass** grade, candidates must complete all tasks and must attain a 98.5% standard of accuracy with no more than 8 presentation errors. A **First Class Pass** will be awarded if candidates achieve a 99% standard of accuracy with no more than 4 presentation errors.

Administration

Prior to the examination, the Specialist Teacher will be expected to prepare and store documents or part documents to be recalled by the candidates during the examination. The Specialist Teacher will also be responsible for assigning names to each candidate's documents and notes about this will accompany the set of papers. At the end of the printing the Specialist Teacher must erase all files from the storage media.

Checklist – Masterclass

		Aided	Date	Unaided	Date
31	**Advanced display** Column work including sort, maths Multi-columns Line draw				
32	**Further editing** Subscript, superscript, composite characters, leader dots Renumbering paragraphs Footnoting, contents and indexing				
33	**Selective mail merge** Merge a standard letter with a datafile selecting against set criteria				
34	**Masterclass examination questions** Ensure that all competences learned in Part 4 meet the required standard for the Masterclass examination				

31 Advanced display

Column work, including sort and maths
Multi-columns
Line draw

At Masterclass level you will be expected to produce complicated tables which need rearrangement. This can be done automatically on some systems using the **sort** facility. If you do not have a sort facility, then you will carefully have to sort the items manually and make sure that they are in the required order. At least with a word processor you can move the items around until they are correct – unlike on a typewriter!

Some of the papers may include columns of figures and this is where you will be able to take advantage of a **maths** or calculator facility to do the calculation for you. Again, if you do not have this function, you will have to do it manually.

You are likely to be asked to put text into 2 or 3 columns in newspaper style. Most business systems can handle this. If your system cannot do this, then you will need to consider upgrading it, since there is no easy way to achieve the result without the facility.

Your ability to draw lines and boxes will be tested at Masterclass level so you need to practise how your system copes with this. You may be asked to draw organisation charts, tick boxes or tables with horizontal and vertical lines, etc.

The following task is taken from a past PEI Examination paper. Please note that in the examination the *recalled task* will have been set up on the candidate's disk by the *tutor*. The first part of this task may therefore be prepared for you by your tutor or you may key in the document yourself.

TASK 1 - *Specialist Teacher to store on disk.*

(Candidate's Name)

TASK 1

SHORT COURSE EXAMINATION RESULTS FOR SUMMER TERM

NAME	BOOK-KEEPING	TYPEWRITING	WORD PROCESSING
Pendleton Grace	PASS	DISTINCTION	PASS
Singh Kashmira	PASS	PASS	PASS
Lindon Barbara	PASS	PASS	PASS
Burns Paula	FAIL	PASS	PASS
Bradley Tracy	DISTINCTION	PASS	PASS
Canning Julie	FAIL	PASS	PASS
Stott Eric	PASS	PASS	PASS
Griffiths Doreen	DISTINCTION	DISTINCTION	DISTINCTION
Carrol Shirley	PASS	DISTINCTION	DISTINCTION
Curtiss Wendy	FAIL	PASS	FAIL
Aston Shirley	FAIL	PASS	PASS
Fitzsimmons Ray	DISTINCTION	DISTINCTION	DISTINCTION
Grant Diane	DISTINCTION	DISTINCTION	DISTINCTION
Ashton Linda	PASS	PASS	PASS
Bi Mohammed	DISTINCTION	DISTINCTION	DISTINCTION

Author's Name: .James Wise......	Task Number ...I................

Create a document: ....   New document name: ....

Edit a document: ......✓...........   Existing document name: ....

Rename document as: ....

Type of copy: Draft: ....   Final: .✓..

Line Spacing: 1 ....   2 ....   As copy: .✓..

No of copies required: ...I........

Paper Size: A4 .✓.   A5 ....   Portrait: ☐   Landscape: ☑

Date Required: ......asap.........   Retain on file: ✓... Delete: ....

SPECIAL INSTRUCTIONS:

Add 2 extra columns to exam list in the order shown by the circled numbers.

U/score column headings.

Sort the full table into alpha order of student.

TASK 1

SHORT COURSE EXAMINATION RESULTS FOR SUMMER TERM — (EMBOLDEN)

NAME	BOOK-KEEPING	TYPEWRITING	WORD PROCESSING	SHORTHAND	OFFICE PRACTICE
Pendleton Grace	PASS	DISTINCTION	PASS	FAIL	PASS
Singh Kashmira	PASS	PASS	PASS Dist.	PASS	PASS
Lindon Barbara	PASS	PASS	PASS	PASS	PASS
Burns Paula	FAIL	PASS	PASS	FAIL	FAIL
Bradley Tracy	DISTINCTION	PASS	PASS	PASS	DISTINCTION
Canning Julie	FAIL	PASS	PASS	FAIL	FAIL
Stott Eric	PASS	PASS	PASS	DISTINCTION	DIST.
Griffiths Doreen	DISTINCTION	DISTINCTION	DISTINCTION	DIST.	DIST.
Carrol/Shirley	PASS	DISTINCTION	DISTINCTION	DIST.	DIST.
Curtiss Wendy	FAIL	PASS	FAIL	FAIL	FAIL
Aston Shirley	FAIL	PASS	PASS	DIST.	DIST.
Fitzsimmons Ray	DISTINCTION	DISTINCTION	DISTINCTION	DIST.	DIST.
Grant Diane	DISTINCTION	DISTINCTION	DISTINCTION	PASS	DIST.
Ashton Linda	PASS	PASS	PASS	PASS	PASS
Bi Mohammed	DISTINCTION	DISTINCTION	DISTINCTION	DIST.	DIST.
①	②	⑤	⑥	④	③

<u>TASK 3</u>

Specialist Teacher to store on disk.

<u>TASK 3</u>   (Candidate's Name)

<u>PRINCIPAL'S BULLETIN</u>

Welcome to this month's Staff Development Newsletter.

In the past, I feel that many Staff have been put off by the apparent complications involved in applying for courses, or have simply not got to know about them.

If you need information about courses, or how to apply, the Staff Development Office is now situated on the first floor of the College in Room 111.

Any help that you may need about courses, applications, claims for travel or expenses, etc, will be available from myself, or the newly-appointed Staff Development Co-ordinator, Miss Lorraine Follows at any time during the week, but specifically, on Fridays between 1.00 pm and 4.30 pm.

It is hoped that all Staff will take advantage of INSET courses which come up during the year, and application is intended to be as simple as possible.

<u>PROCEDURE</u>

Whether you see a course advertised on the Staff Development Notice Board, through these Newsletters, or from your own endeavours, your first point of contact is your HOD. Your HOD will sanction attendance on bona fide courses. You then simply go to the Staff Development Co-ordinator for the appropriate forms - I promise the procedure is very uncomplicated.

Please remember though, that covering your classes is of prime importance and you will have to arrange that through your HOD. Where cover <u>is</u> required, then replacement costs are available. All we need to know in addition is:

who is covering for the member of Staff on a course
the day, date and times
subject(s)
grade of the course.

Grades are normally IV and V, and your replacement will be paid at the appropriate rate.

WORD PROCESSING REQUEST FORM

Author's Name: ...*Principal*.........	Task Number ...3............

Create a document:	New document name: ....

Edit a document: ....✓...........	Existing document name: ....
	Rename document as: ....

Type of copy: Draft:	Final: ..✓..

Line Spacing: 1 .✓.. 2	As copy: ....

No of copies required: ....

Paper Size: A4 .✓.. A5	Portrait: ☑	Landscape: ☐

Date Required: ...*asap*.........	Retain on file: ..✓.. Delete: ....

SPECIAL INSTRUCTIONS:

Please re-print this draft bulletin in 2 columns as shown with justified right-hand margin.

Col 1

PRINCIPAL'S BULLETIN ← (BOLD)   (2 LINES OF SPACE)

Welcome to this month's Staff Development Newsletter.

In the past, I feel that many Staff have been put off by the apparent complications involved in applying for courses, or have simply not got to know about them.

If you need information about courses, or how to apply, the Staff Development Office is now situated on the first floor of the College in Room 111.

Any help that you may need about courses, applications, claims for travel or expenses, etc, will be available from myself, or the newly-appointed Staff Development Co-ordinator, Miss Lorraine Follows, at any time during the week, but specifically, on Fridays between 1.00 pm and 4.30 pm.

It is hoped that all Staff will take advantage of INSET courses which come up during the year, and application is intended to be as simple as possible.

PROCEDURE ← (BOLD)   (2 LINES OF SPACE)

your

Whether you see a course advertised on the Staff Development Notice Board, through these Newsletters, or from your own endeavours, your first point of contact is your HOD. Your HOD will sanction attendance on bona fide courses. ~~You~~ then ~~simply~~ uc go to the Staff Development Co-ordinator for the appropriate forms - I promise the procedure is very uncomplicated.

Col 2

Please remember though, that covering your classes is of prime importance and you will have to arrange that through your HOD. Where cover is required, then replacement costs are available. All we need to know in addition is:

who is covering for the member of Staff on a course
the day, date and times
subject(s)
grade of the course.

Grades are normally IV and V, and your replacement will be paid at the appropriate rate.

Change 'Newsletter' to 'Bulletin' and 'HOD' to 'Section Head' please across both columns
Main hdg. centred in bold 'BROOKFIELD COLLEGE NEWS'

The following task is taken from a past PEI Examination paper. Please note that in the examination the *recalled task* will have been set up on the candidate's disk by the *tutor*. The first part of this task may therefore be prepared for you by your tutor or you may key in the document yourself.

TASK 1

Specialist Teacher to store on disk. Key-in as displayed ensuring that the text on the next page is in double-line spacing.

TASK 1   *(Candidate's Name)*

Welcome to the Self Help Plan; a plan that lets you learn about your attitudes, thoughts and feelings towards food in a very special way. Through a series of quizzes you will learn new ways to reshape old eating habits.

The Self Help Plan is an important part of the Shape-Up formula for success. While the Food Plan deals with what you eat, and the Exercise Plan shows you how you can exercise to enhance your (wieght) loss, the Self Help Plan concentrates on how you relate to food and eating. Each of these aspects of losing weight, together with the support you get from your class, will help you achieve your target - (safley) and effectively.

You will find the questions you've asked yourself time and again are answered:

how can I manage special occasions without overeating?
how can I control my favourite foods◯
how can I cope with shopping and cooking?
how do my moods affect my eating?
how do I develop my willpower?

Perhaps a little voice inside you is concerned whether you really can lose weight. In fact, your belief in your ability to do what it (take) to lose weight is a very important ingredient for success. You can win, whether this is your first attempt to lose weight or you've tried many times before.

We all know that in order to lose weight and keep it from creeping back, we have to change our habits. The first step is to (to) discover which of those habits and feelings about eating are helpful, and which are harmful to your efforts in losing weight.

Each of us has different weight loss goals and different eating habits to change. Yet we all have one thing in common. At some point we reached our last straw and said to ourselves: "That's it. I've got to lose weight."

There's no need to wait until you reach target weight for you to reap the (benifits) of weight loss success.

Every change you make during your efforts to lose weight is an (acomplishment.) Since the rewards of a slim body take time to achieve, giving yourself rewards along the way (boost) your motivation to stay with the Self Help Plan.

SPECIALIST TEACHER PLEASE NOTE

The above is a proof-reading task. To aid your preparation the "deliberate mistakes" are circled and care should be taken to ensure that errors are repeated when this document is created.

Begin by giving yourself short-term rewards after you accomplish short-term goals, such as exercising and/or staying on the Food Plan all day. You can also plan for long-term rewards after accomplishing weekly or monthly goals, such as keeping to the Plan for a week or losing a specific amount of weight.

Then reward yourself with something you really like - some new make-up, a new video, a new LP, a fishing trip, a day out.

WORD PROCESSING REQUEST FORM

Author's Name: ..SILVIA ADAMS... *Course Leader*	Task Number ..../.............
Create a document:	New document name: ....
Edit a document: ......✓............	Existing document name: ....
	Rename document as: ....
Type of copy: Draft: .... Final: .✓..	
Line Spacing: 1 ..✓ 2 .... As copy:	
No of copies required:	
Paper Size: A4 .✓. A5 .... Portrait: ☑ Landscape: ☐	
Date Required: ...Asap...... Retain on file: .✓. Delete:	

SPECIAL INSTRUCTIONS:

Insert as a footer:

SHAPE UP SELF HELP PLAN
in CAPS and Right Aligned.

Justify RHM of continuous text.

enjoyable

Welcome to the Self Help Plan; a plan that lets you learn about your attitudes, thoughts and feelings towards food in a very special way. Through a series of quizzes you will learn new ways to reshape old eating habits.

vital

The Self Help Plan is an ~~important~~ part of the Shape-Up formula for success. While the Food Plan deals with what you eat, and the Exercise Plan shows you how you can exercise to enhance your wieght loss, the Self Help Plan concentrates on how you relate to food and eating. Each of these aspects of losing weight, together with the support you get from your class, will help you achieve your target – safley and effectively.

that   *over*

You will find the questions/you've asked yourself ~~time and~~ again are answered: (leave 2 clear linespaces)

Inset ½"

how can I manage special occasions without overeating?
how can I control my favourite foods
how can I cope with shopping and cooking?
how do my moods affect my eating?
how do I develop my willpower?

(leave 2 clear linespaces)

Perhaps a little voice inside you is concerned whether you really can lose weight. In fact, your belief in your ability to do what it take to lose weight is a very important ingredient for success. You can win, whether this is your first attempt to lose weight or you've tried many times before.

: this time you won't give up

We all know that in order to lose weight and keep it from creeping back, we have to change our habits. The first step is to to discover which of those habits and feelings about eating are helpful, and which are harmful to your efforts in losing weight.

Each of us has different weight loss goals and different eating habits to change. Yet we all have one thing in common. At some point we reached/~~our~~ last straw and said to ourselves: "That's it. I've got to lose weight."

the

There's no need to wait until you reach ~~target weight for you to reap the benifits of weight loss success.~~

of

Every change you make during your efforts to lose weight is an acomplishment. Since the rewards of a slim body take time to achieve, giving yourself rewards along the way boost your motivation to stay with the Self Help Plan. *This, in turn, boosts yr. Confidence.*

This, in fact, can bring feelings of hope th. can help us feel differently about ourselves. Along w. losing weight, we plan for other changes th. are full of exciting possibilities. Keep these feelings in mind & you too will become a WINNER

Sgl.
LSP.

Begin by giving yourself short-term rewards after you accomplish short-term goals, such as exercising and/or staying on the Food Plan all day. You can also plan for long-term rewards after accomplishing weekly or monthly goals, such as keeping to the Plan for a week or losing a specific amount of weight.

Then reward yourself with something you really like - ~~some~~ new ⚡/ make-up, a new video, a new LP, a fishing trip, a day out.

Understanding Your Excuses ← (Caps + Centre)

Have you ever told yourself th. you were buying sweets or biscuits for the children or because you were expecting visitors, when really you <u>knew</u> they were for you? We've all done this, but now it's time to deal with excuses directly.

NEW
PAGE

To recognise what kinds of excuses you make & how often, read the list below. Once you recognise them you can deal w. them.

Tick <u>one</u> of the boxes on the right.

	OFTEN	SOMETIMES	NEVER
1 I am buying this food for someone else	☐	☐	☐
2 I'll go back on the diet plan tomorrow	☐	☐	☐

3 I'll order the full meal but I'll only take a taste

4 I don't want to feel left out when the others are eating

5 I need this sweet to give me energy

6 I'm cooking this for my friends

7 I can't be rude and not eat when they've made it for me

8 I've been good I deserve a treat

Copy boxes down

The following task is taken from a past PEI Examination paper. Please note that in the examination the *recalled task* will have been set up on the candidate's disk by the *tutor*. The first part of this task may therefore be prepared for you by your tutor or you may key in the document yourself.

TASK 3

Specialist Teacher to store on disk.

TASK 3   (Candidate's Name)

NUTRIENT PROFILES

(PROTIEN)

Helps build and repair all body (tisssues.)
Assists in forming antibodies which fight infection.
Supplies energy.

Fish, poultry, lean meat, eggs, cheese, milk, peas and beans,
peanut butter.

CARBOHYDRATE

Supplies energy.
Supplies fibre.

Bread, cereals, peas and beans, pasta, rice, fruits.

FAT

Supplies (essentail) fatty acids.
Carries fat-soluble vitamins.
Supplies energy.

Vegetable oils, margarine, mayonnaise.

VITAMIN A

Helps keep skin clear and smooth.
Helps keep mucous membranes and inner linings of the body
healthy and resistant to infection.
Essential to enable the eyes to adjust to dim light.

CALCIUM

Helps in producing and maintaining strong bones and healthy
teeth.
Helps in blood clotting and in the healthy functioning of the
nervous system.

Milk, cheese, canned fish, green vegetables (leafy), beans,
prawns, yoghurt.

SPECIALIST TEACHER PLEASE NOTE

*The above is a proof-reading task. To aid your preparation the
"deliberate mistakes" are circled and care should be taken to ensure that
errors are repeated when this document is created.*

WORD PROCESSING REQUEST FORM

Author's Name: ..Silvia Adams.... Task Number ..3...............

Create a document: .... New document name: ....

Edit a document: ....✓............. Existing document name: ....

Rename document as: ....

Type of copy: Draft: .... Final: .✓..

Line Spacing: 1 .✓.. 2 .... As copy: ....

No of copies required: ...✓.......

Paper Size: A4 .✓.. A5 .... Portrait: ☐ Landscape: ☑

Date Required: ...Asap........ Retain on file: .✓.. Delete: ....

SPECIAL INSTRUCTIONS:

Reformat in two columns as shown below, inserting the headings.

NUTRIENT PROFILES

What They Do For You   Food Sources

PROTEIN

Helps build and repair all   Fish, poultry, lean meat,
body tissues _ _ _ _ _ _ _ _   eggs _ _ _ _ _ _ _

CARBOHYDRATE _ _ _ _ _ _   Bread, Cereals _ _ _

Balance the columns appropriately please

NUTRIENT PROFILES

Col 1

PROTIEN

Helps build and repair all body tisssues.
Assists in forming antibodies which fight infection.
~~Supplies~~ energy. Provides ↖

Col 2

Fish, poultry, lean meat, eggs, cheese, milk, peas and beans,
peanut butter.

CARBOHYDRATE

Provides
~~Supplies~~ energy.
Supplies fibre.

Bread, cereals, peas and beans, pasta, rice, fruits.

FAT

Supplies essentail fatty acids.
Carries fat-soluble vitamins.
~~Supplies~~ energy. Provides ↖

Vegetable oils, margarine, mayonnaise.

VITAMIN A

Helps keep skin clear and smooth.
Helps keep mucous membranes and inner linings of the body healthy and
resistant to infection.
~~Essential to enable the eyes to adjust to dim light.~~

CALCIUM

Helps in producing and maintaining strong bones and healthy teeth.
Helps in blood clotting and in the healthy functioning of the nervous
system.

Milk, cheese, canned fish, green vegetables (leafy), beans,
prawns yoghurt.

Carrots, pumpkins, spinach, greens, broccoli, cantaloupe melon,
apricots, peaches, milk, liver, margarine.

VITAMIN C
Strengthens body tissues. [Helps formation of bones & teeth.
Increases resistance to infection. [Promotes healing. Helps to
adsorb iron.

Oranges, grapefruit, strawberries cantaloupe melon, honeydew melon,
mango, papaya; kiwi fruit, green peppers, Brussels sprouts, broccoli,
potatoes, tomato juice.

Check your success

Did you format your text into 2 columns? ☐

Did you achieve a balanced appearance? ☐

Did you print on A4 landscape paper? ☐

Did you carry out the editing functions correctly? ☐

Did you correct the deliberate mistakes 'protien', 'tisssues' and 'essentail'? ☐

32 Further editing

Use subscript, superscript, composite characters, leader dots
Renumber paragraphs
Use automatic footnoting, contents and indexing facilities

In addition to testing all the features covered in the Advanced Word Processing syllabus, at Masterclass level you are expected to be able to use more automatic functions. These include the functions listed above. They will not be tested in every paper, but you should know how to handle each function on your particular system.

A **subscript** or inferior character is one that prints below the normal typing line; a **superscript** or superior character is a character which prints above the normal typing line:

H_2O m^2

Overprinting is used to print two or more characters on top of each other to form a composite character:

overprint tete and ˆ to make tête

Leader dots are used to take the eye along a table. A continuous line of dots can be used, or they can be typed in groups. Always make sure that you leave at least one clear space at each end of the line and make sure that the spacings are consistent:

eg   Office furniture $5400
      Software $7900

When paragraphs are moved, inserted or deleted, then the numbering will be incorrect. Some word processing systems can automatically number paragraphs. If yours can, then use it – otherwise you will have to be very careful to ensure that you do not make a mistake if you renumber paragraphs manually.

Producing footnotes, contents pages and an index are automatic features that are invaluable if you are typing a long report, dissertation, book, etc. You should not find it difficult to do these functions and they can be very time-saving.

A selection of these functions is illustrated in the tasks on the following pages.

The following task is taken from a past PEI Examination paper. Please note that in the examination the *recalled task* will have been set up on the candidate's disk by the *tutor*. The first part of this task may therefore be prepared for you by your tutor or you may key in the document yourself.

TASK 2

Specialist Teacher's copy - key in with ragged right-hand margin, on two separate pages, following the line-spacing as shown.

TASK 2   *(Candidate's Name)*

OVERVIEW This year saw the successful completion of our first Medical Secretarial Course. The first year students have also maintained excellent (attendnace) and we (forsee) no drop out rate as they progress to their second year. It is also encouraging that we have had many enquiries for the start of courses in September. This, I feel, is in no small part due to the superlative marketing strategy of the Course Team. Moreover, the College Open Day last year brought the Course to the attention of many potential clients. Our students did a splendid PR job and much of the credit for raising awareness levels in the Medical Secretarial field belongs to them.

MARKETING Several photographs taken by our Marketing Manageress whilst the students were on Field Work will be appearing in the next edition (fo) the College Prospectus. This will be a welcome advertisement for the Course as naturally, we had no such pictures previously.

JOB PLACEMENTS It is very gratifying that over 50 per cent of
Field Work placement providers were so impressed with our
students that they have been offered permanant position on
successful completion of the Course. The remaining Medical
Secretaries have also obtained full time and part time
positions, which means that we have achieved 100 per cent job
placement after our 'first attempt'. Naturally, this also
provides excellent motivation for the first year students as
they can verify that their hard work has a very good chance of
being rewarded with a permanent job at the end of it.

ENROLMENTS For this year's new intake, we have 11 firm
enquiries from students who fulfil the entry criterea. In
addition, we have 2 students from a former Short Corse at this
College. I include their Course results below.

Their Course Tutor assures me that these are reliable, puntual,
and trustworthy students who are keen to embarque on a carreer
in the Medical Secretarial field. We will be making provision
for them on the Course.

Their presence should prove a valuable resource for the new
students as they are 'old hands' and know their way around the
College and the Annexe.

WORD PROCESSING REQUEST FORM

Author's Name: ..Sally Jones....	Task Number ...2...............

Create a document:	New document name: ....

Edit a document: .....✓..........	Existing document name: ....
	Rename document as: ....

Type of copy:	Draft:	Final: .✓..

Line Spacing: 1	2	As copy: .✓..

No of copies required: ...!.......	
Paper Size: A4 .✓.. A5	Portrait: ☑ Landscape: ☐

Date Required: ..asap.........	Retain on file: .✓.. Delete: ....

SPECIAL INSTRUCTIONS:

Retrieve this report. Insert header - Medical Secretarial Course - in caps on every page & centred. Number pages bottom centre. Justify right-hand margin. All paragraph headings to shoulder headings in bold.
Print one copy.

(Candidate's Name)

> PLEASE CHECK
> MY SPELLINGS!

OVERVIEW   This year saw the successful completion of our first

Medical Secretarial Course.   The first year students have also

maintained excellent attendnace and we forsee no drop out rate

as they progress to their second year.   It is also encouraging

that we have had many enquiries for ~~the start of/courses~~ in   *↲ stet*

September.   ~~This, I feel, is in no small part due to the~~   *↲*

~~superlative marketing strategy of the Course Team.~~   Moreover,   *↲*

the College Open Day last year brought the Course to the

attention of many potential clients.   Our students did a

splendid PR job and much of the credit for raising awareness

levels in the Medical Secretarial field belongs to them.

Move
to
'A'

MARKETING   Several photographs taken by our Marketing

Manageress whilst the students were on Field Work will be

appearing in the next edition fo the College Prospectus.   This

will be a welcome advertisement for the Course as

naturally, we had no such pictures previously.

uc

INDUCTION
Having the second year students involved in the induction of the new
intake during enrolment week proved to be benificial in allaying
fears in the 1st year group & in answering problems from first-hand
experience. The same induction programme will take place this year.
This becomes increasingly important after the field work in hospitals
& clinics when these students provide valuable feedback to their
colleagues.

> *Display in double*
> *line spacing, except*
> *where instructed otherwise*

JOB PLACEMENTS   It is very gratifying that over ~~50~~ 60 per cent of Field Work placement providers were so impressed with our students that they have been offered permanant position on successful completion of the Course.   The remaining Medical Secretaries have also obtained full/time and part/time positions, which means that we have achieved 100 per cent job placement after our 'first attempt'.   Naturally, this also provides excellent motivation for the first year students as they can ~~verify~~/that their hard work has a very good chance of being rewarded with a permanent job at the end of it.

ENROLMENTS   For this year's new intake, we have 11 firm enquiries from students who fulfil the entry criterea.   In addition, we have 2 students from a former Short Corse at this College.   I include their Course results below.

Their Course Tutor assures me that these are reliable, puntual, and trustworthy students who are keen to embarque on a carreer in the Medical Secretarial field.   We will be making provision for them on the Course.

Their presence should prove a valuable resource for the new students as they are 'old hands' and know their way around the College and the Annexe.

Insert data on Mohammed Bi and Tracy Bradley as shown:

INSET FROM LHM in sgl. line Sp.

Mohammed Bi

Tracy Bradley

List Subjects

List Results

'A'

There wl. be an in-service, Course Team Staff Dev. day towards the end of next nth.. I ~~will~~ shall be calling a team mtg. w. you in two weeks time to discuss the programme & venue. Personally, I feel we shd. get 'off-site,' and hold the event either at the Teachers' Centre or at the Golden Pheasant Htl.. This latter venue was used successfully by the B TEC Course Team recently. I shall circulate further details shortly.

Linda Prestwich
— CURRICULUM LEADER

The following task is taken from a past PEI Examination paper. Please note that in the examination the *recalled task* will have been set up on the candidate's disk by the *tutor*. The first part of this task may therefore be prepared for you by your tutor or you may key in the document yourself.

TASK 2

Specialist Teacher to store on disk.

TASK 2   (Candidate's Name)

Success for everyone

MODULE 1

Our Food Plan shows you how you can eat three (sastisfying) meals, plus snacks each day and still lose (weigth.)

MODULE 2

You'll progress with expanded food choice - more to eat, new (menues,) more variety.

MODULE 3

You will have an even greater food choice and different menus. The Self Help Plan will begin (guilding) you towards a lifetime of (succesful) weight management.

MODULE 4

The Food Plan Diary is the one you will carry with you until you reach your target weight. You'll learn to (adopt) the Food Plan to your specific needs, and you'll also learn about good (nutritoin) along the way.

SPECIALIST TEACHER PLEASE NOTE

The above is a proof-reading task. To aid your preparation the "deliberate mistakes" are circled and care should be taken to ensure that errors are repeated when this document is created.

WORD PROCESSING REQUEST FORM

Author's Name: ..*SILVIA ADAMS*...	Task Number ..*2*...............

Create a document:	New document name: ....

Edit a document: ......*✓*...........	Existing document name: ......·....
	Rename document as: ....

Type of copy: Draft:	Final: .*✓*..

Line Spacing: 1 ..*✓*. 2	As copy: ....

No of copies required: ....*1*......	
Paper Size: A4 .*✓*. A5	Portrait: ☑ Landscape: ☐

Date Required: ..*Asap*.........	Retain on file: ..*✓* Delete: ....

SPECIAL INSTRUCTIONS:

All headings, (except Main Hdg.) to side headings

Please change MODULE (s) TO WEEK (s)

Success for everyone ⟶ (Caps + block to body of text)

↕ leave 1 clear linespace only

MODULE 1

Our Food Plan shows you how you can eat three sastisfying meals, plus snacks each day and still lose weigth.

MODULE 2

will

You'll progress with ~~expanded~~ *greater* food choice - more to eat, new menues, more variety.

MODULE 3

You will have an even greater food choice ~~and different monus.~~

The Self Help Plan will begin guilding you towards a lifetime of succesful weight management.

MODULE ~~4~~ 5

The Food Plan Diary is the one you will carry with you until you reach your target weight. You'll learn to adopt the Food Plan to your specific needs, and you'll also learn about good nutritoin along the way.

Module 4 still more, new foods and recipe ideas to make the Food Plan even more enjoyable. In this module, we also introduce our Exercise Plan which includes exercise for everyone, and at a level to suit your life-style.

Modules 6 to 12 You will rec. four Menu Plans + 3 life Style leaflets. The leaflets cover PicFnic lunches, Dining Out, Family uc Meals, and Special Occassions. They will help you to cope with these situations + still lose weight.

Progress

As you continue to attend your Shape-Up mtgs., you receive important weight-loss support Materials.

Follow-On Our Special Follow-On Plan helps you stay at yr. target weight using the skills + techniques you hv. learnt in reaching it.

Check your success   Did you use capital letters and blocked style for the main heading?   ☐

Did you make all other headings into side headings?   ☐

Did you change 'MODULE' to 'WEEK' and 'Modules' to 'WEEKS'?   ☐

Did you join up 'Picnic' and put 'Lunches' not 'lunches'?   ☐

Did you expand all abbreviations?   ☐

Did you correct all errors?   ☐

Selective mail merge

Merge a standard letter with a datafile selecting against set criteria

At Advanced level you were asked to merge a standard document with a pre-stored datafile and produce documents for each record on the datafile. At Masterclass level you may be asked to set up and key in your own datafile and then create your standard letter. You will next have to select only certain records and merge the standard letter with the datafile to produce personalised letters for some of the records. An additional complication will be that the datafiles will be of different lengths and you may have to type an extra field for the salutation.

Example

Please produce the following datafile and print one copy.

```
Mr A Rose                This record has one less field
3 Falkirk Street         in the address than the next record.
Montrose
Scotland
3 months

Mrs T Roberts            Both records must be typed in such
23 Haslingden            a way that you can send a letter
Blackwood                to Mr Rose and Mrs Roberts.
Melbourne
South Australia
6 months
```

Practice from the paper

The following task is taken from a past PEI Examination paper.

WORD PROCESSING REQUEST FORM

Author's Name: .Pamela. Hunt......	Task Number ..4...............
Create ⚡ document**s**	New document name: ....
Edit a document:	Existing document name: .... Rename document as: ....
Type of copy: Draft:	Final: .✓..
Line Spacing: 1 .✓.. 2	As copy: ....
No of copies required: .!. of. each.	
Paper Size: A4 .✓.. A5	Portrait: ☑ Landscape: ☐
Date Required: .today..........	Retain on file: .✓. Delete: ....

SPECIAL INSTRUCTIONS:

Key-in the following datafile & print one copy on either portrait or landscape A4 paper.

Key-in the standard letter & print one copy for all the local firms in Liverpool. Use Ref PL/yr. initials & a ragged right-hand margin.

Mr J Hall
Managing Director
BLS Office Machines
Unit 12
Britonwood Trading Estate
LIVERPOOL
L32 8BJ

Mr S Post
Kelco Biospecialities Ltd.
Penrhyn Road
Knowesly Industrial Est.
LIVERPOOL
L34 6XJ

Mrs C Patel
Cross International
Knowesly Ind. Est.
LIVERPOOL
L42 9BJ

Miss R Solado
Fareway Transport Co. Ltd.
London St.
SOUTHPORT
Merseyside
PR6 8LM

Ms P O'Shea
Homelink Ltd.
27 High St.
SOUTHPORT
Merseyside
PR6 3LM

Mr S Macdonald
ADS Ltd.
Parker St.
ST HELENS
Merseyside
WA4 3PT

Dear

The students and staff cordially invite you to an Open Day at
Brookfield College on the first Thursday of next month. ✳

We hope that the Open Day will give you the opportunity to see
the sort of work that we are currently undertaking at the
College with a view to providing future employees for your
organisation.

May we also point out that the College is always available to
deliver courses for your own staff and management. We believe
that we are at the leading edge in the field of flexible
training for updating in computer studies - word processing,
desk top publishing, computer aided design, spreadsheet
processing and database management.

Please bring along any questions you may have with regard to
training, day release courses and open learning. Our staff and
students will be only too pleased to answer your queries.

lc   *We hope to have the pleasure of your company at the*
        ⟨_Buffet lunch⟨is included ~~with~~ your invitation, *and will be served in the*
               which   *in*   *conference from noon*
We look forward to seeing you and discussing your needs,   *onwards.*
present and future.

Yours sincerely

Pamela Lunt
(Marketing Manager)

✳ *The Open Day starts at 0930 hrs with registration. Coffee and
biscuits will be provided on yr. arrival. The Principal will make a
short welcome address at approx. 1000 hours. By this time you will
hv. been allocated a guide who will be happy to escort you to those
areas of the college of interest to the company.*

Practice from the paper

The following task is taken from a past PEI Examination paper.

WORD PROCESSING REQUEST FORM

Author's Name: .. *Silvia Adams* ...	Task Number ..... *4* ....
Create a document (s)	New document name: ....
Edit a document:	Existing document name: .... Rename document as: ....
Type of copy: Draft:	Final: .✓..
Line Spacing: 1 .✓.. 2	As copy: ....
No of copies required: ...*3*...... Paper Size: A4 .✓.. A5	Portrait: ☑ Landscape: ☐
Date Required: .*TOMORROW*....	Retain on file: .✓.. Delete: ....

SPECIAL INSTRUCTIONS:

Produce a Mailshot for members who completed the course 3 months ago.

Use margins of 1½" left, 1" right

Ragged RHM please

Ref is author's inits./yr. inits.

You may print the datafile on portrait or landscape paper.

Dear

FOLLOW - ON PLAN -(BOLD)

Congratulations on successfully completing the Shape-Up weight loss programme. [As you know, it is our policy to keep track of our members after they hv. finished their course. It is now * since you achieved yr. target weight, and we shd. like to know how you are progressing.

Please reply using the SAE enclosed, and don't forget: you are most welcome to come in and visit us anytime. Our present members wd. be very interested to talk with you.

Best wishes for yr. future health & happiness.

Yours etc.

Please produce the following datafile and print one copy.

Mr A Carter
2 Saxon Way
Rhyll
Clwyd
LL5 6OP

3 months

_____

Miss G Waring
19 School Lane
Didsbury
Manchester
M14 9LD

6 Months

_____

Miss L Roberts
42 Oak Crescent
Warrington
WA5 7UY

3 Months

_____

Mrs E Byrne
279 Chapel St.
Southport
PR21 4EL

12 Months

_____

Ms R Hackett
16 Delph Close
Wigan
WA13 1PJ

6 Months

_____

Mr S Yeates
17 St Domingo Grove
Liverpool
L4 9XJ

3 Months

_____

Check your success   Did you type the datafile so that you can easily identify the salutation?   ☐

Did you print the datafile?   ☐

Did you remember to date the letter?   ☐

Are your margins the sizes specified?   ☐

Did you remember not to justify the right margin?   ☐

Did you produce 3 correct letters?   ☐

34 Masterclass examination questions

There now follows a Masterclass Examination paper, which has been worked through and solutions provided.

If you wish, you may work through the paper yourself before comparing your printout with the solutions.

Please note that these are model answers only and in no way do they carry the authority of the Examining Board. However, in order to tackle the tasks in conditions which mirror examination conditions, it will be necessary for your **Specialist Teacher** to set up those tasks which need to be stored on disk prior to the commencement of the examination paper.

Further practice

For further practice, copies of past papers can be obtained from PEI. It is suggested that you practise working through as many papers as possible before taking the examination.

Note: For further helpful hints, *see* **Section 35 Preparing for the Word Processing examinations**.

This paper must be returned
with the candidates' work.
Failure to do so will result in
delay in processing the
candidates' scripts.

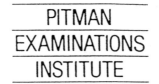

```
┌──────────────────────────────────┐
│                                  │
│                                  │
│  WORD PROCESSING - MASTERCLASS   │
│                                  │
│                                  │
│                                  │
└──────────────────────────────────┘
```

No.

Instructions for Invigilators

1 **Before the Examination**

1.1 Give each candidate an Entry Form and ensure that it is completed fully.

1.2 Tell the candidates what arrangements they should follow for the printing out of their documents. NB: The time taken for printing must not be included in the total time for this examination (2 hours 10 minutes).

1.3 Tell the candidates to follow page format instructions.

1.4 Tell candidates that after the examination tasks have been handed out they may not communicate with each other in any way. If they wish to speak to the Invigilator they must hold up their hand, but the Invigilator may not answer any question about the content of the paper or the operation of the system during the examination.

1.5 Hand out the sets of tasks (Question Paper).

1.6 Tell candidates that they have 10 minutes to read through the tasks in silence, during which time they may make notes, but may not operate the word processor.

1.7 Begin timing 10 minutes' reading time.

2 **The Examination**

2.1 At the end of the reading time tell candidates that they may start work, and begin timing the examination.

2.2 At the end of 2 hours, tell candidates that they must stop work, and file the document which they have on the screen.

3 **After the Examination**

3.1 Collect the sets of tasks (Question Paper) from each candidate.

3.2 Supervise printing out of documents in the formats required, reminding candidates that they may make no alterations to the contents of documents at this stage, and may not communicate with each other until the printing is completed.

3.3 Collect printout, checking that the candidate's name appears on every page submitted, and ensuring that each candidate's work is securely stapled together, in correct sequence (or left in continuous form if fanfold paper is used). If candidate's name has been omitted, this should be inserted in ink by the Invigilator, and initialled.

3.4 Ensure that documents are erased from storage medium.

3.5 Sign Attestation Form, and attach copies of documents prepared by Specialist Teacher for the use of candidates.

WORD PROCESSING - MASTERCLASS

PITMAN
EXAMINATIONS
INSTITUTE

No.

To be handed to Specialist Teacher before the date of the examination

This pack contains:

One Specialist Teacher's instructions and details of Tasks to be created on storage medium.

1   In advance of the date of the examination, you are asked to create documents on the storage medium for the attached tasks.

2   You may key in text using character line length for 10-pitch or 12-pitch.

3   Please follow the text exactly (including "deliberate mistakes").

4   Copies of these documents should be created on the storage medium for the exclusive use of each individual candidate.

5   Because word processing systems vary so widely between Centres it is not possible for the Examiner to specify file names for documents. Please allocate suitable file names for the documents created (TASK 1, TASK 2, etc are suggested, as appropriate). Likewise, please devise suitable file names for candidates to store their completed tasks.

6   Please complete the spaces provided on each of the WORD PROCESSING REQUEST FORMS, or as otherwise indicated, so that these file names will be available to candidates at the start of the examination.

7   The preparation of all examination material must be regarded as strictly confidential and should be carried out under the supervision of the Invigilator. No details of the content of the examination may be divulged, and the Specialist Teacher and Invigilator are asked to sign the Attestation Form to this effect. This should be enclosed with the worked scripts, together with a printed specimen copy of each of the prepared tasks.

8   All material must be erased from the system and storage medium at the end of the examination after the completion of all the required printing.

<u>*TASK 1*</u>   *(Candidate's Name)*

CHLP

This year (mark) the 25th (anniversay) of the opening of Copley Hall to the public and as a result of increased activity we are pleased to be able to offer the following attractions - many of which are new for this year.

Copley Hall

Historic Copley Hall is one of (Yorkshires) finest mansions built (originaly) in the late 16th century but expanded by the Chambers family during the (ninteenth) century. The Hall combines the best of both periods in both its (achitecture) and its interior design and furnishings. In fact it is hard to imagine another house where two such contrasting periods are so perfectly in balance with each other. Set in beautiful gardens, the house is a veritable treasure-trove to those who enjoy seeing beautiful antiques in a real setting.

Copley Mill

Founded in 1784 this was one of the first (water-poewred) mills for spinning wool. Over 60 apprentices, often (children) worked these machines to produce thread used by the weavers and this was one of the pioneering methods of the factory system.

Today with the help of money from a private (truat) fund, the mill has been restored to full working order and again you can experience what it must have been like to be one of the early workers.

Next to the Copley Mill is the Chambers Mill, built a few years later (that) Copley Mill to house the mechanised weaving frames. Here you can see how the spun thread is processed into finished cloth.

Copley Kitchen

Housed in the former stables of the Hall, is a restaurant and cafeteria serving food and drink all day long while the CHLP is open. The adjacent Mill Shop sells a variety of gifts including (legnths) of unbleached cloth spun and woven at CHLP.

Copley Country Park

Much of the estate was built for the mill owners and their workers. There are many miles of woodland walks along the narrow wooded valley with the stream rushing in the bottom. Stop at the many viewing places and try to spot some of the many varieties of bird and small mammal that live in these woods.

(continued)

TASK 1 (continued)

How to get to CHLP

By road take the B3254 from Huddersfield towards Oldham and follow the signposts.

By rail Copley station is about half an (hours) pleasant walk from the CHLP.

SPECIALIST TEACHER PLEASE NOTE

To aid your preparation the "deliberate mistakes" are circled and care should be taken to ensure that errors are repeated when this document is created.

TASK 3   (Candidate's Name)

COPLEY HALL CRAFT SUPPLIES
(leave 2 line spaces)

(PROCE) LIST

(leave 2 line spaces)

SWIVEL CUTTER   General purpose knife
FILIGREE BLADE   steep angle for deep cutting
HAIR BLADE   Marks hair textures
EMBOSSING WHEEL   Complete with 3 wheels
FOIL - GOLD   3/8" wide x 400 ft
FOIL - SILVER
STAMPS   Chrome-plated, hand-finished
RAWHIDE MALLET   Heavy rawhide head, wooden handle
LEATHER STAIN   6 colours, 50 ml bottles
LEATHER LACQUER   Cellulose-based, waterproof
LIQUID WAX   Dries in 3-5 mins, then buff
TONER   Highlights carving
THONGING CHISEL   Tempered steel
EYELETS   Internal diameter
PUNCH PLIER   Revolving

```
SPECIALIST TEACHER PLEASE NOTE

To aid your preparation the "deliberate mistakes" are circled and care
should be taken to ensure that errors are repeated when this document is
created.
```

<u>TASK 4</u>   *(Candidate's Name)*

LEATHER WORKING COURSES

Leather can be one of the most rewarding materials to work with and lends itself to many objects both useful and ornamental. It is easy to work with once the foundations have been mastered and, unlike (comercially) made products, it is not expensive to do.

Numerous courses (is) available at Copley Hall (thorughout) the winter months from October to April. A variety of (tehcniques) is demonstrated by experts and courses are organised to cater for all levels of ability and interest. (Course's) vary in length so (that) should be one to suit both your availability and your standard.

The courses (hald) at Copley Hall attract expert teachers from all over the world to supplement our resident tutor, Cora McDonald. The following programme is for the coming year.

All courses are residential. (Acommodation) is in the (luxurous) surroundings of Copley Hall itself.

Costs are £80 per day (which includes) all accommodation, meals and tuition.

Sample materials are provided for the first project then any materials can be purchased if required.

WINTER SCHEDULE OF COURSES

The following standard courses are planned. Others may be organised by request or at short notice.

1a Making fashion garments - introduction
1b Making fashion garments - experienced

2   Fastening and decorating techniques

3   Painting dyeing and finishing

4a Tooling and carving - introduction
4b Tooling and carving - experienced

SPECIALIST TEACHER PLEASE NOTE

To aid your preparation the "deliberate mistakes" are circled and care should be taken to ensure that errors are repeated when this document is created.

WORD PROCESSING - MASTERCLASS

This paper must be returned
with the candidate's work,
otherwise the entry will be void
and no result will be issued.

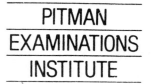

No.

CANDIDATE'S NAME ....
(Block letters please)

CENTRE NO. ....DATE ....

This examination lasts for 2 hours and consists of four
tasks which you should file on the storage medium for
printing out later. The Invigilator will give you
instructions about arrangements for printing out your
documents.

You have 10 minutes to read through the tasks and documents
before starting the examination. Check that you have been
given all the document names required to create, recall or
store your finished work.

_____

FOR EXAMINER'S USE ONLY

COMPLETION	ACCURACY	DISPLAY

<u>CANDIDATE'S INSTRUCTIONS</u>

You work as the Secretary to the Chairman,
Michael Garlick, of Copley Hall Leisure Park,
Copley Wood, HALIFAX HX2 7PR.

Please complete the following tasks from your
in-tray taking care to proof-read and correct
any errors.

———————————

WORD PROCESSING REQUEST FORM

Author's Name: M. Garlick	Task Number 1
Create a document:	New document name:
Edit a document: ✓	Existing document name:
	Rename document as:
Type of copy: Draft: ✓	Final: ....
Line Spacing: 1 .... 2 ✓	As copy: ....
No of copies required: 1	
Paper Size: A4 ✓ A5	Portrait: ☑ Landscape: ☐
Date Required: a.s.a.p	Retain on file: ✓ Delete: ....

SPECIAL INSTRUCTIONS:

Please up-date our leaflet according to the attached amendments. Print it in double - line spacing with a justified right-hand margin.

Expand CHLP throughout.

Header top left CHLP (in full) - Caps.

Number pages bottom centre.

(Candidate's Name)

Embolden all headings + put into caps

CHLP

leave 3" (7.5cm) here for Map

This year mark the 25th anniversary of the opening of Copley Hall to the public and ~~as a result of increased activity~~ we are pleased to be able to offer the following attractions - many of which are new for this year.

Copley Hall

Historic Copley Hall is one of Yorkshires finest mansions built originaly in the late 16th century but expanded by the Chambers family during the ninteenth century. The Hall combines the best of both periods in both its achitecture and its interior design and furnishings. In fact, it is hard to imagine another house where two such contrasting periods are so perfectly in balance with each other. Set in beautiful gardens, the house is a veritable treasure-trove to those who enjoy seeing beautiful antiques, ~~in a real~~ *in their original* setting.

Copley ~~Mill~~ *and Chambers Mills*
            Copley Mill

Founded in 1784 ~~this~~ was one of the first water-poewred mills for spinning wool. Over 60 apprentices, often children, worked these machines to produce thread used by the weavers ~~and this was one of the pioneering methods of the factory system~~. *This factory was one of the first pioneers moving wool spinning away from cottages.*
Today with the help of money from a private truat fund, the mill has been restored to full working order and again you can experience what it must have been like to be one of the early workers.

Next to the Copley Mill is ~~the~~ Chambers Mill, built a few years later that Copley Mill to house the mechanised weaving frames. Here you can see how the spun thread is processed into finished cloth.

Copley Kitchen

Housed in the former stables of the Hall, is a restaurant and cafeteria serving food and drink all day long while the CHLP is open. The adjacent Mill Shop sells a variety of gifts including legnths of unbleached cloth spun and woven at CHLP.

Copley Country Park

Much of the estate was built for the mill owners and their workers. There are many miles of woodland walks along the narrow wooded valley with the stream rushing in the bottom. Stop at the many viewing places and try to spot some of the many varieties of bird and small mammal that live in these woods.

How to get to CHLP

indent

By road take the B3254 from Huddersfield towards Oldham and follow the signposts.

By rail Copley station is about half an hour's pleasant walk from the CHLP.

Insert at A*

OPENING TIMES AND DATES

	OPEN	CLOSED	TIMES
COPLEY HALL	4 July - 15 August	Every Friday	1100 - 1645 hrs
COPLEY + CHAMBERS	"	" "	1100 - 1630 hrs
MILLS			
COPLEY COUNTRY PARK	1 May - 30 Sept	"	1000 - 1800 hrs

COPLEY KITCHEN

COPLEY MILL SHOP   ⟨Details as Copley Hall above⟩

Free car and coach parking

For details of the specialist leather working courses plse. see the sep. leaflet.   caps

Entry Fees
Hall £2
Mills £1·50
Park £1

⟨Do not use ditto marks⟩

WORD PROCESSING REQUEST FORM

Author's Name: .M .Garlick............	Task Number .2....................
Create ✗ document(s)...... ✓..........	New document name: ....
Edit a document:	Existing document name: ....
	Rename document as: .... ⁄.
Type of copy:　　　Draft: ....　　Final: .✓..	
Line Spacing: 1 .✓..　　2 ....　　As copy:	
No of copies required: .1.of.each...	
Paper Size: A4 .✓..　　A5 ....　　Portrait: ☑　　Landscape: ☐	
Date Required: .today..........	Retain on file: .✓.. Delete: ....

SPECIAL INSTRUCTIONS:

Please Key-in the datafile and print one copy, either portrait or landscape.

Please send a copy of the letter to those on the datafile who are life members.

Mr + Mrs L Clark
The Hough
43 Chestnut Drive
Pudsey
BRADFORD
W Yorkshire
BD3 7LR
Family

Mr + Mrs T Emmerson
Water Cottage
High Street
HOLMFIRTH
W Yorkshire
HD4 3XL
Family

Mr + Mrs S Iwanowski
271 Cousin Lane
SOWERBY BRIDGE
W Yorkshire
HX6 3LR
Life

Mr + Mrs P Schofield
96 Castle Carr Avenue
West Houghton
WAKEFIELD
W Yorkshire
WF3 9RU
Life

Mr + Mrs N Kobita
4 Victoria Street
Clifton
BRADFORD
W Yorkshire
BD4 3ST
Life

Mr + Mrs B Bi
24 Victoria Drive
Northowram
BRADFORD
W Yorkshire
BD3 1SN
Family

Dear   Ref MG/your initials

SPECIAL VISIT TO COPLEY HALL [underline]

[2nd Wed next Month]

In order to commemorate 25 years of opening the Hall to the public, there wl. be a special opening day on * for those of our patrons who are Life Members.

Colonel + Mrs Colin Chambers wl. show you around their home + wl. put on view areas of the Hall th. are not usually open to the public. These wl. include the display of fine Jacobean furniture in the Drawing Room + early examples of English porcelain. In addition it wl. be poss. to visit the Library where pictures + tapestries of Pepys + Evelyn can be seen. These are usually not shown to the public as bright light can fade the colours.

The visit wl. end with afternoon tea taken in the Orchid conservatory. Here you can browse thro' many diff. specimens of orchids that hv. been grown in the nurseries of the Hall. There will be opportunity to purchase plants at the estate shop at the conclusion of the tour if you wish, although it is stressed that there wl. be no pressure placed on you to purchase anything.

The visit is from 2pm to 5pm + the cost per person is £4.

(continued)

I should be grateful if you wd. return the completed slip so that we can reserve a place as numbers wl. be restricted to 70.

Yours etc.

MG
Chairman

- -

2nd Wed next mth

I should like _____ tickets for the visit on ✳ and I enclose a cheque for £   made payable to Copley Hall Ltd.

Name -

Address -

- - - - - - - - - Postcode - - - - - - - - -

Telephone No. - - - - - - - - - - -

Author's Name: .M. Garlick..........	Task Number ..3...................
Create a document:	New document name: ....
Edit a document: ......✓...........	Existing document name: ....
	Rename document as: ....
Type of copy: Draft: .... Final: .✓..	
Line Spacing: 1 .... 2 .... As copy: .✓..	
No of copies required: ...!........	
Paper Size: A4 .✓.. A5 .... Portrait: ☐ Landscape: ☑	
Date Required: ..asap..........	Retain on file: .✓.. Delete: ....

SPECIAL INSTRUCTIONS:

Amend the table as shown. Sort into alphabetical order of items + print one copy.

COPLEY HALL CRAFT SUPPLIES
[leave 1 linespace only]

PRICE LIST
[Centre & bold]

*A

ITEM	DESCRIPTION	PRICE EACH £ Qty 1-5	Qty 6+	CODE
SWIVEL CUTTER	General purpose knife	2·45	2·45	S197
FILIGREE BLADE	Steep angle for deep cutting	1·80	1·35	B206
HAIR BLADE	Marks hair textures on leather	1·90	1·50	B911
EMBOSSING WHEEL	Complete with 3 wheels	2·95	2·45	W350
FOIL - GOLD	3/8" wide x 400 ft	3·50	3·00	F101
FOIL - SILVER	" " " "	3·50	3·00	F102
STAMPS	Chrome-plated, hand-finished	2·50	2·15	P66-P127
RAWHIDE MALLET	Heavy rawhide head, wooden handle	6·85	6·00	R142
LEATHER STAIN	6 colours, 50 ml bottles	1·85	1·60	L915
LEATHER LACQUER	Cellulose-based, waterproof (1 litre)	3·25	2·95	L916
LIQUID WAX	Dries in 3-5 mins, then buff 500 ml	2·40	1·75	L814
TONER	Highlights carving 500 ml	1·80	1·60	T319
THONGING CHISEL	Tempered steel	2·35	2·15	C124
EYELETS	Internal diameter ⅜" (100)	4·00	3·50	E503
PUNCH PLIER	Revolving head	1·95	1·65	P149

[Complete as above]

*[Move to *A]*

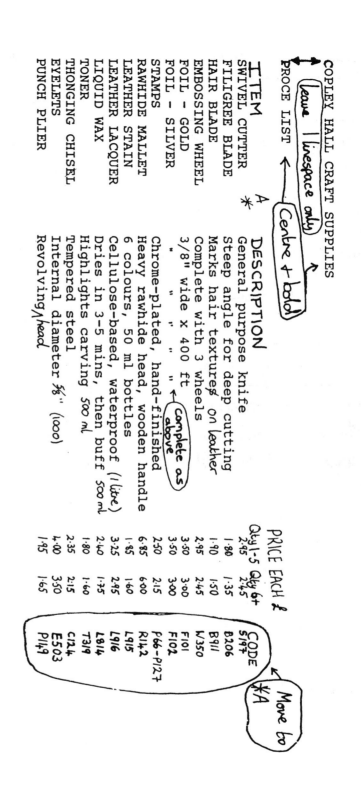

Author's Name: M. Garlick .... Task Number .4. ....

Create a document: .... New document name: ....

Edit a document: .....✓.............. Existing document name: ....

Rename document as: ....

Type of copy: Draft: .... Final: .✓..

Line Spacing: 1 .... 2 .... As copy: .✓..

No of copies required: ...1........

Paper Size: A4 .✓.. A5 .... Portrait: ☐ Landscape: ☑

Date Required: ..asap.......... Retain on file: .✓. Delete: ....

SPECIAL INSTRUCTIONS:

Please correct the draft copy + follow the amendments.
Please re-format it into 2 columns as indicated.

LEATHER WORKING COURSES [*basic techniques*] [*↑ the making of*]

Leather can be one of the most rewarding materials to work with and lends itself to many objects both useful and ornamental. It is easy to work with once the ~~foundations~~ have been mastered and, unlike comercially made products, it is not expensive to do.

Numerous courses is available at Copley Hall thorughout the winter months from October to April. A variety of tehcniques is demonstrated by experts and courses are organised to cater for all levels of ability and interest. Course's vary in length so that should be one to suit both your availability and your standard.

The courses hald at Copley Hall attract expert teachers from all over the world to supplement our resident tutor, Cora McDonald. ~~The following programme is for the coming year.~~

All courses are residential. Acommodation is in the luxurous surroundings of Copley Hall itself.

[*including*]
Costs are £80 per day ~~which includes~~ all accommodation, meals and tuition.

~~Sample materials are provided for the first project then any materials can be purchased if required.~~

WINTER SCHEDULE OF COURSES

The following standard courses are planned. Others may be organised by request or at short notice.

[*column 2*]

1a	Making fashion garments - introduction	6-9 Oct., 16-19 Feb.
1b	Making fashion garments - experienced	22-26 Nov., 12-16 Mar.
2	Fastening and decorating techniques	2-4 Oct., 12-14 Dec., 1-3 Apr.
3	Painting dyeing and finishing	5-9 Dec., 22-26 Feb.
4a	Tooling and carving - introduction	4-8 Nov., 11-15 Feb.
4b	Tooling and carving - experienced	9-15 Jan., 1-7 Mar.

[*leave a clear linespace between all numbered courses.*]

[*months in full please.*]

COPLEY HALL LEISURE PARK

<u>TASK 1</u>   (Candidate's Name)

COPLEY HALL LEISURE PARK

This year marks the 25th anniversary of the opening of Copley Hall to the public and we are pleased to be able to offer the following attractions - many of which are new for this year.

COPLEY HALL

Historic Copley Hall is one of Yorkshire's finest mansions built originally in the late 16th century but expanded by the Chambers family during the 19th century. The Hall combines the best of both periods in both its architecture and its interior design and furnishings. In fact, it is hard to imagine another house where 2 such contrasting periods are so perfectly in balance with each other. Set in beautiful gardens, the house is a veritable treasure-trove to those who enjoy seeing beautiful antiques in their original setting.

1

COPLEY HALL LEISURE PARK

COPLEY AND CHAMBERS MILLS

Founded in 1784, Copley Mill was one of the first water-powered mills for spinning wool. Over 60 apprentices, often children, worked these machines to produce thread used by the weavers. This factory was one of the first pioneers moving wool spinning away from cottages.

Today, with the help of money from a private trust fund, the mill has been restored to full working order and again you can experience what it must have been like to be one of the early workers.

Next to the Copley Mill is Chambers Mill, built a few years later than Copley Mill to house the mechanised weaving frames. Here you can see how the spun thread is processed into finished cloth.

COPLEY COUNTRY PARK

Much of the estate was built for the mill owners and their workers. There are many miles of woodland walks along the narrow wooded valley with the stream rushing in the bottom. Stop at the many viewing places and try to spot some of the many varieties of birds and small mammals that live in these woods.

COPLEY KITCHEN

Housed in the former stables of the Hall is a restaurant and cafeteria serving food and drink all day long while the Copley Hall Leisure Park is open. The adjacent Mill Shop sells a variety of gifts including lengths of unbleached cloth spun and woven at Copley Hall Leisure Park.

2

COPLEY HALL LEISURE PARK

OPENING TIMES AND DATES

	OPEN	CLOSED	TIMES
COPLEY HALL	4 July-15 August	Every Friday	1100-1645 hours
COPLEY AND CHAMBERS MILLS	4 July-15 August	Every Friday	1100-1630 hours
COPLEY COUNTRY PARK	1 May-30 September	Every Friday	1000-1800 hours
COPLEY KITCHEN	4 July-15 August	Every Friday	1100-1645 hours
COPLEY MILL SHOP	4 July-15 August	Every Friday	1100-1645 hours

Entry Fees

Hall £2.00

Mills £1.50

Park £1.00

Free car and coach parking

For details of the specialist Leather Working courses please see the separate leaflet.

HOW TO GET TO COPLEY HALL LEISURE PARK

By road: take the B3254 from Huddersfield towards Oldham and follow the signposts.

By rail: Copley station is about half an hour's pleasant walk from the Copley Hall Leisure Park.

3

TASK 2

Mr and Mrs L Clark,The Hough,43 Chestnut Drive,Pudsey,BRADFORD,W Yorkshire,BD3 7LR,Mr and Mrs Clark,Family
Mr and Mrs T Emmerson,Water Cottage,High Street,HOLMFIRTH,W Yorkshire,HD4 3XL,Mr and Mrs Emmerson,Family
Mr and Mrs S Iwanowski,271 Cousin Lane,SOWERBY BRIDGE,W Yorkshire,HX6 3LR,Mr and Mrs Iwanowski,Life
Mr and Mrs P Schofield,96 Castle Carr Avenue,West Houghton,WAKEFIELD,W Yorkshire,WF3 9RU,Mr and Mrs Schofield,Life
Mr and Mrs N Kobita,4 Victoria Street,Clifton,BRADFORD,W Yorkshire,BD4 3ST,Mr and Mrs Kobita,Life
Mr and Mrs B Bi,24 Victoria Drive,Northowram,BRADFORD,W Yorkshire,BD3 1SN,Mr and Mrs Bi,Family

4

For reasons of space, only one of the 4 letters is reproduced here. Candidates must ensure they submit all letters required.

TASK 2   (Candidate's Name)

Ref MG/aa

24 October 1992

Mr and Mrs S Iwanowski
271 Cousin Lane
SOWERBY BRIDGE
W Yorkshire
HX6 3LR

Dear Mr and Mrs Iwanowski

SPECIAL VISIT TO COPLEY HALL

In order to commemorate 25 years of opening the Hall to the public, there will be a special opening day on Wednesday 11 November 1992 for those of our patrons who are Life Members.

Colonel and Mrs Colin Chambers will show you around their home and will put on view areas of the Hall that are not usually open to the public. This will include the display of fine Jacobean furniture in the Drawing Room and early examples of English porcelain. In addition it will be possible to visit the Library where pictures and tapestries of Pepys and Evelyn can be seen. These are usually not shown to the public as bright light can fade the colours.

The visit will end with afternoon tea taken in the Orchid conservatory. Here you can browse through many different specimens of orchids that have been grown in the nurseries of the Hall. There will be opportunity to purchase plants at the estate shop at the conclusion of the tour if you wish, although it is stressed that there will be no pressure placed on you to purchase anything.

The visit is from 2 pm to 5 pm and the cost per person is £4.

I should be grateful if you would return the completed slip so that we can reserve a place as numbers will be restricted to 70.

Yours sincerely

Michael Garlick
Chairman

I should like ____ tickets for the visit on Wednesday 11 November 1992 and I enclose a cheque for £   made payable to Copley Hall Ltd.

Name _____

Address _____

_____ Postcode _____

Telephone Number _____

TASK 3

(Candidate's name)

COPLEY HALL CRAFT SUPPLIES

PRICE LIST

ITEM	CODE	DESCRIPTION	PRICE EACH £	
			Qty 1-5	Qty 6+
EMBOSSING WHEEL	W350	Complete with 3 wheels	2.95	2.45
EYELETS	E503	Internal diameter 5/8" (1 litre)	4.00	3.50
FILIGREE BLADE	B206	Steep angle for deep cutting	1.80	1.35
FOIL - GOLD	F101	3/8" wide x 400'	3.50	3.00
FOIL - SILVER	F102	3/8" wide x 400'	3.50	3.00
HAIR BLADE	B911	Marks hair texture on leather	1.90	1.50
LEATHER LACQUER	L916	Cellulose-based, waterproof (1 litre)	3.25	2.95
LEATHER STAIN	L915	6 colours, 50 ml bottles	1.85	1.60
LIQUID WAX	L814	Dries in 3-5 mins, then buff (500 ml)	2.40	1.75
PUNCH PLIER	P149	Revolving head	1.95	1.65
RAWHIDE MALLET	R142	Heavy rawhide head, wooden handle	6.85	6.00
STAMPS	P66-P127	Chrome-plated, hand-finished	2.50	2.15
SWIVEL CUTTER	S197	General purpose knife	2.95	2.45
THONGING CHISEL	C124	Tempered steel	2.35	2.15
TONER	T319	Highlights carving (500 ml)	1.80	1.60

TASK 4

LEATHER WORKING COURSES

Leather can be one of the most rewarding materials to work with and lends itself to the making of many objects both useful and ornamental. It is easy to work with once the basic techniques have been mastered and, unlike commercially made products, it is not expensive to do.

Numerous courses are available at Copley Hall throughout the winter months from October to April. A variety of techniques is demonstrated by experts and courses are organised to cater for all levels of ability and interest. Courses vary in length so there should be one to suit both your availability and your standard.

The courses held at Copley Hall attract expert teachers from all over the world to supplement our resident tutor, Cora McDonald. All courses are residential. Accommodation is in the luxurious surroundings of Copley Hall itself.

WINTER SCHEDULE OF COURSES

Costs are £80 per day including all accommodation, meals and tuition.

The following standard courses are planned. Others may be organised by request or at short notice.

1a   Making fashion garments - introduction
     6-9 October, 16-19 February

1b   Making fashion garments - experienced
     22-26 November, 12-16 March

2   Fastening and decorating techniques
     2-4 October, 12-14 December, 1-3 April

3   Painting, dyeing and finishing
     5-9 December, 22-26 February

4a   Tooling and carving - introduction
     4-8 November, 11-15 February

4b   Tooling and carving - experienced
     9-15 January, 1-7 March

35 Preparing for the Word Processing examinations

Thinking about examinations is always intimidating. It can create unpleasant feelings of panic, even in well prepared candidates. For those who are less well prepared the temptation is to avoid this feeling by thinking about or doing almost anything else. However you should remember that you are not alone in these feelings and that other people have successfully overcome them to pass examinations.

The first lesson to learn is not to allow yourself any excuses for putting off exam preparation. If you have been able to complete the tasks in this guide to an adequate standard you are well on the way. This guide can be used to undertake a **skills and knowledge audit** in preparation for the examinations, so that by being *honest with yourself* you can discover and correct any deficits which may trip you up on the day.

Never concentrate merely on those areas in which you are confident and know you are competent: look for **weaknesses** as well as **strengths**. Even if the result of your audit is favourable you should recognise that the format of the examinations, while being designed to test your word processing skills under some pressure (probably a fair representation of some of the common crises that may be found in the real workplace), will offer some opportunities and threats. You need to be *familiar with the examination requirements and practise satisfying them under the time and other constraints* that you will face. **Examination technique** must be added to word processing skills. During this process do not forget that other candidates and those who have delivered this course for you can provide a useful, positive source of support.

Time constraints

Make sure that you have allowed yourself sufficient time *before* the examination date to practise *past papers* in conditions that are as near to the real examination as possible. **Do not delay** doing this. Remember that you will *print out* completed tasks *after the examination* and that *no alterations are allowed to the contents of tasks* at this time. You may print out any task during the examination to check for errors. However, you should **proof-read tasks carefully onscreen** and **store them on disk**.

Your invigilator will hand out the examination tasks, after which you must *not* communicate with other candidates. There is a **reading through period** during which time you may make notes but you must not operate your system. **Use this time well**. Have a *highlight* pen ready for highlighting instructions – eg *use double line spacing* or *use right justification*. Check that your instructions include the file names under which the recalled tasks have been filed by your specialist teacher.

Syllabus

Read the examination syllabus carefully for your examination. Is there anything that you do not understand?

Skills and knowledge audit

If you have maintained an accurate **checklist record** while carrying out the exercises and tasks in this guide, then you probably have a good idea of your own word processing **strengths** and **weaknesses**. As well as referring to the checklist, have a look at the results of your practice papers. Perhaps you marked them or perhaps they were marked by your specialist teacher. Use the following guide and draw up a list of your errors. Do they fall mainly into the category of **accuracy** errors or is your **presentation** weak?

Accuracy

Spelling
Typographical
Missing word
Extra word
Missing phrase or sentence
Extra phrase or sentence
Reference omitted
Incorrect salutation
Incorrect date

Incorrect address
Incorrect close to letter
UC instead of LC
LC instead of UC
Letters transposed
Block move **retyped**
    incorporating **further errors**
Failure to correct **proof-reading**
    errors

Presentation

Margins
Incorrect layout
Incorrect line spacing
Poor pagination
Incorrect centring
Incorrect underscore
Incorrect emboldening

Inconsistent spacing of columns
Inconsistent alignment of
    columns
Inconsistency of **style of
    presentation** within document
Mixture of ragged right and
    right justification

Examiners' reports

Another source of helpful information in preparation for the examinations is the report of the examiners. Your tutor should have access to a copy and will be able to guide you in where common errors occur.

Finally

Good luck! If you prepare well and have sufficient practice, you should be successful in your examinations.

Appendix – business documents

1.1 Business letter Fully blocked style, open punctuation

```
                    CONTEXT CONFERENCES
                    International House
                         High Street
                           EALING
                           London
                           W5 5DB

            Tel:  01-597-4267   Fax:  01-840 621
```

Date (day, month, year) ← 5 May 19..

URGENT → *Nature of document*

→ *Letterhead (writer's address)*

→ *One clear line-space between items*

Receiver's address (Addressee) ←
Mr J Bricknell
Rhinefield House
Brockenhurst
Hants
SO42 7QB

Salutation ← Dear Mr Bricknell

Subject heading ←
CATERING IN THE 1990S
THURSDAY 15 MAY THE COBURG HOTEL LONDON

Body of letter

Further to your telephone call I confirm that one place has been reserved for you at the above conference as requested.

Please find enclosed details showing how to get to the Coburg Hotel. On arrival make your way to the Queensway Suite where you will receive your delegate badge.

Registration will take place between 10 am and 10.30 am when coffee will also be served.

Should you arrive late there will be a number of reserved seats at the back of the conference room for you to occupy.

Delegates may have messages left for them on the hotel's main telephone number 01-229 3654, quoting the Catering in the 1990s conference.

Please let me know as soon as possible should you require a vegetarian meal at lunchtime.

I look forward to meeting you at the conference.

← *One clear line-space between paragraphs*

Closing Co. Name
Yours sincerely *(Complimentary close)*
CONTEXT CONFERENCES LTD

← *Sufficient space for signature*

Writer's name and job title
Lynn Farmer
Conference Manager *(designation)*

Enc

Enclosure

1.2 Memorandum

Fully blocked style, open punctuation

M E M O R A N D U M → *Example of* <u>spaced</u> *capitals*

To   Personnel

From   Martin Short } *Clear line space between items*

Date   10 May 19..

Please find attached a copy of the advertisement that will
appear in The Advertiser on Wednesday 15 May.

If you take a call, please ask:

name, address, school/college leaver or with personnel
experience.

Enc

1.3 Report

Any material that is in paragraph form (apart from a letter) is typed following the rules
used for reports. Manuscripts, minutes, news releases and articles are examples of work
classified as reports.

There now follows an example of an 'extract' from a report which is typed in blocked
style.

<u>**HOW TO PROOF-READ**</u> → *centred heading using bold + underscore*

Proof-reading is the process of finding and correcting
errors. All the work you produce must be carefully checked
to ensure accuracy. Even the most experienced worker will
make mistakes.

<u>Proof-reading procedures</u> → *heading above paragraphs called* SHOULDER *heading*

When you check your work, you must read the copy twice -
once for accuracy of each word, looking for spelling,
punctuation and spacing errors. The second reading is for
thought content - whether the group of words together makes
sense. Each individual word may be correct, but a use of
language error may exist. Look at this example:

One clear line Space between paragraphs →

We trust ∧ find the adjustment satisfactory. *^you will*

The missing words 'you will' before 'find' cause the whole
sentence to be wrong, even though each word by itself is
correct.

Compare the work you are checking against the original
continually as you proof-read. If you are in any doubt,
consult the author. Do not make changes that alter the
meaning of the text.

Using a word processor, copy should be proof-read before it
is printed. Make it a habit to proof-read each screenload
before scrolling to the next screen.

Accurate proof-reading is a skill that is learned and
developed through practice and it is a skill that is highly
prized by all employers.

The MINUTES of the ANNUAL GENERAL MEETING of the BRANCH
held at 7 pm on Thursday 19 May 19X1 in the Hamtun Suite of
the Southampton Park Hotel, Cumberland Place, Southampton.

PRESENT   A B Hayes (Chairman)
              K A Mountford (Vice Chairman)
              I P Chapel (Treasurer)
              R A West (Vice Chairman Elect)
              J K Spruce (Secretary)
              47 members of the Branch as Attendance Record

APOLOGIES FOR ABSENCE were received from 6 members as
listed in the record.

1   <u>**MINUTES**</u>   — *Headings - bold, closed caps & underscore*

Body of text aligned with position of shoulder headings

The Minutes of the Annual General Meeting held on 14
May 19X0 were received, approved and signed by the
Chairman as a true record of the proceedings.

2   <u>**CHAIRMAN'S REPORT**</u>

The Chairman presented his Report to the Branch for
the year 19X1/X2.   The Report was received and
approved.

3   <u>**FINANCIAL REPORT**</u>

The Treasurer presented his audited accounts for the
year ended 31 March 19X1 and explained the
significance of items detailed therein.   The Meeting
unanimously received and adopted the Accounts for the
year to 31 March 19X1 and they were then signed by
the Chairman.

4   <u>**BRANCH OFFICERS**</u>

The Chairman announced that Dr George Brown would be
invited to become the first Branch President.   The
role would be honorary with no executive status.

5   <u>**ANY OTHER BUSINESS**</u>

6   The Meeting closed at 7.25 pm.

1.5 Display

The two examples below illustrate 2 common methods of displaying text

ONE OF THESE WILL BE YOURS

A brand new Austin Metro Car

Centre longest line →| Hand-made Dartington Lead Crystal

A VHS Video Recorder

Type every line from this starting point

A Motor Driven Disc Camera

A Compact Disc Player

£500 Cash

A Microwave Oven

ONE OF THESE WILL BE YOURS

A brand new Austin Metro Car

Hand-made Dartington Lead Crystal

A VHS Video Recorder

Centre each line

A Motor Driven Disc Camera

A Compact Disc Player

£500 Cash

A Microwave Oven

1.6 Simple table

The example below shows the typical layout of material which is set out in columns, using a blocked style of display within each column.

HYDRAULIC PROOF PRESSURE TEST — *Centred heading*

'TCH SIZE	SAMPLE SIZE	ACCEPTABLE NO
91–	1	0
151–280	2	0
	2	0
		0
		0
		0
		0

equal space columns